THE PHILI...
Debt and Poverty

Rosalinda Pineda-Ofreneo

Oxfam

A catalogue record for this book is available from
the British Library

ISBN 0 85598 149 0
ISBN 0 85598 150 4 pbk

Published by Oxfam UK and Ireland, 274 Banbury Road, Oxford OX2 7DZ
Designed by Jeffrey Meaton OX 583 JM 91
Printed by Oxfam Print Unit
Typeset in 10pt Palatino

CONTENTS

Foreword

It is commonly assumed that the international debt crisis is so complex that it should be left to economists to solve. Perhaps, however, we have relied for too long on 'experts' to address the problem. The debt crisis has not abated: indeed, it is getting worse. Agencies like Oxfam, working alongside the poor in countries like the Philippines, daily witness the human suffering caused by the enormous debts owed by their governments to financial institutions in the 'developed' world.

Poverty at national level soon permeates down to the level of the poorest and most vulnerable. The burden of the debt contracted by the government of the Philippines is borne by the poor, who pay for it in terms of reduced incomes, and the under-funding of the health and education services on which they depend. In stark terms, the debt leads to deprivation and marginalisation, wasted lives and even death.

Some observers may question why a charitable agency like Oxfam involves itself in the debate on the international debt crisis. Charities, it might be argued, should concentrate on development projects and on the direct relief of suffering. Of course, such work is Oxfam's primary mandate – a mandate which is fulfilled in the Philippines by our continuing support for such projects as training programmes in fishing communities, literacy work and credit funds for women in shanty towns, income-generation schemes with tribal people, and reconstruction work in disaster-stricken areas.

But if 'regular' development and relief work serves to maintain the myth of a net flow of resources from the relatively rich North to the relatively poor South, we feel we have an obligation to point out the error of such an assumption. The fact is that, in terms of the flow of resources, the South is actually supporting the North. The issue of debt is central to this inverted (or perverted) 'development'. To cite just one example: for the past two years, Oxfam UK/Ireland has devoted an average of about £300,000 a year, donated by the British and Irish public, to development and relief efforts in the Philippines. By the standards of non-governmental organisations, this is a considerable amount – but really only a drop in the ocean, when compared with funds allocated by the Philippine government to debt payment. During 1990 the average payment of interest (not actual repayment!) on the country's debts amounted to about £3 million *a day*. The daily interest payment on the debt incurred for the controversial Bataan Nuclear Power Plant, mothballed since President Aquino came to power, amounts to almost £200,000 a day.

Not all debt payment goes overseas; it is true that nowadays much of the burden of Philippine debt is due to domestic borrowing. Still, much of the domestic debt was and is being incurred to enable the Philippine government to buy foreign exchange to pay for its international borrowing: a roundabout way of paying for the same thing. It is also true that debt is not by any means the sole cause of all the problems afflicting poor people in the Philippines; nevertheless, the burden of the national debt aggravates the whole range of difficulties which they have to cope with daily.

In reflecting on its experience of working with poor communities, Oxfam has come to appreciate the crucial significance of the debt problem. We support the research work of the Freedom From Debt Coalition, a broad-based Filipino network of church groups, academic and professional bodies, and community organisations, which studies the social and environmental impact of debt, to try to find solutions to the crisis which will ease poverty and suffering in the Philippines.

The perverse flow of resources from South to North is one factor impelling concern by agencies such as Oxfam. But an equally powerful factor is the increased pressure on them to deliver services that the Philippine government can no longer provide. (The administration of President Aquino is allocating about 40 per cent of its budget to debt service – a higher proportion than the British government allocates to spending on defence, social security, welfare, and housing combined.) But charities should never assume the role of governments. Non-governmental organisations can never even contemplate being able to compensate for what national ministries can no longer provide: such things as affordable medical care, fair salaries for teachers, and investment in basic infrastructure.

The Philippine government has so far opted to repay the nation's debt 'as a matter of honour', and at all costs. The stories in this book give some idea of what those costs are in human terms – and what grassroots organisations in the Philippines are trying to do to reduce them.

Paul Valentin
Oxfam UK/Ireland Representative, Manila
July 1991

Acknowledgements

Rene Ofreneo, Dean of the School of Labour and Industrial Relations at
the University of the Philippines, contributed to Chapters 6 and 7 of this
book. Vincent Homolka, an independent researcher and economist
working with the Development Policy Unit of Oxfam UK and Ireland,
wrote the concluding chapter, to add a Northern perspective on measures
which international creditors might take to help to solve the debt crisis in
the Philippines. The Philippine Resource Centre in London helped to
compile details of contacts and resources. The author gratefully
acknowledges all these contributions.

1

Introduction

Margie Amblon is now childless. Her two small children died of measles and its attendant complications, one after the other. In her poor community, like many other urban communities in the Philippines, there is no health centre. ... Carolina Agustin, a domestic helper in Kuwait, came home to the Philippines in September 1989 with her two feet in plaster. The reason: she jumped from a window when her employer tried to rape her. Another domestic worker, Emelieta Edrosolan, returned to the Philippines in April, exhibiting black welts on her thighs from beatings by her employer.[1] ... Lupo Masaclao used to be a fisherman living off the bounty of Laguna Lake. Now that the lake is dying and being diverted to uses other than fishing, he has turned into a shoemaker, together with most fisherfolk in his community. ... Up north, in the Cordilleras, the indigenous peoples of Itogon have mounted human barricades to stop open-pit mining operations that would tear up the mountains and destroy the sources of their livelihood. ... In the centre of Manila, the laundrywomen of Tondo eke out a precarious existence from a monthly income of P300 (£6.25), even while trying to learn how to read and write.

Margie Amblon's children could have been saved if there were a health centre in their community. But servicing the nation's foreign debt, which at one point took up almost half the national budget, prevents the government from providing such facilities. Carolina Agustin might perhaps not have ventured to work abroad for an abusive employer had the debt problem not driven the government to encourage the export of labour at whatever cost. Lupo Masaclao and the indigenous peoples of Itogon would perhaps not be threatened by pollution and the destruction of mountains and forests had the environment not been sacrificed for the sake of debt-connected and dollar-oriented 'development'. The laundry-women of Tondo would not be in such desperate straits had they not been afflicted by widespread unemployment, rampant inflation, housing problems, and lack of basic social services, all of which are directly linked to the debt crisis.

All these people are victims of a raging debt crisis which takes most of its toll on the poor and the vulnerable. They are paying the price of a debt policy which puts creditors first and people last. The government of the Philippines has adopted a debt-fuelled model of development that is based on earning cash by exploiting its human and natural resources, some of them irreplaceable.

The Philippines is a country rich in resources. So why are at least half of its 62 million people poor?[2] The answer lies partly in the wealth that is taken from the country in the form of debt service. When the foreign debt was at its peak of $28 billion in 1988, the debt burden of each Filipino man, woman, and child was estimated at P10,000 (£208.33). Even the unborn are already indebted. But this burden is not equitably shared, because in the final analysis, the poor pay more in terms of higher prices and increased taxes for basic goods and services. Their wages stagnate or barely rise in the midst of rapid inflation, as the peso devalues and erodes their purchasing power. They have less access to social services, because the government is too short of cash to provide proper services. Yet they are earning dollars for their country, either by being obliged to work in export production, or by remitting money from better-paying jobs abroad.

Because they are the most affected by the debt crisis, the poor and vulnerable are driven to respond to it in a new and effective way. People's initiatives, exemplified by the Freedom From Debt Coalition and other action-oriented organisations dealing directly or indirectly with the debt issue, have devised novel and alternative approaches that could prove viable and sustainable in the long run.

The people of the Philippines cannot wait. Their country needs immediate debt relief. The extensive devastation wrought by the earthquake of July 1990 (which killed 1,600 people, injured 3,200, made over 100,000 homeless, and damaged property worth £305 million), and the eruption of the volcano Mount Pinatubo in June 1991 (which caused even more damage) makes a solution to the problem of the debt crisis an urgent necessity.

2

The origins of the problem

The Philippines is aspiring to be a Newly Industrialising Country (NIC) like Taiwan, South Korea, Malaysia, and Thailand who are her neighbours in East Asia. The reality is that this is just a severely indebted country, ranking sixth (after Brazil, Mexico, Argentina, Venezuela, and Thailand) in the World Bank Debt Tables for 1989-1990.[1]

Being a severely indebted country means being in a state of perpetual financial haemorrhage. For the Philippines, debt service for 1990 totalled $4.719 billion, more than a billion dollars higher than the $3.670 billion recorded in 1989. Because more money has gone out of the country as interest and principal payments than has come in as 'new money', negative net resource outflows or transfers have been building up. In the years 1988-1990 these totalled a minus of $6.893 billion.[2]

Such a debilitating outflow robs the people of resources that could go into economic recovery and development, basic utilities and social services, and structural reforms to empower the poor and spur sustainable development. What is worse, the people pay for the outflow in terms of new taxes exacted by the government to earn more revenues for debt service. They work harder and longer, but earn less real income, due to devaluation and inflation that stem from policies demanded by the nation's creditors. The people shoulder much of the debt-service burden through the dollars they remit from overseas employment, into which they have been forced by debt-connected structural unemployment and underemployment. The continuing export of Filipinos to help pay the debt, despite the loneliness, uncertainty and humiliation they often suffer, is perhaps the worst effect of the debt crisis.

Future generations will suffer from the environmental degradation accelerated by the debt problem. Only one-fifth of Philippine forests is left, due partly to massive exportation and smuggling of logs and other forest products for the sake of generating desperately-needed foreign exchange.[3] Whole mountains are being torn up, and formerly productive rivers and lakes are being destroyed by export-oriented gold and copper mines and other industries. Only one quarter of Philippine coral reefs is in good condition, and fisheries production has dropped by half as a result of the use of cyanide, dynamite and other destructive forms of fishing.[4]

Chris Daniel/Oxfam

Logs from the tropical rainforest of Quezon Province being loaded on board ship at Real. Illegal logging is a major problem.

Debt-connected poverty has driven fisherfolk to resort to such desperate methods, even as the landless rural poor try to eke out a living by encroaching farther and farther into forest lands. If current trends continue, Philippine forests will completely disappear within this decade, which will mean ever more disastrous floods, droughts, and landslides.

This indeed is a 'fate worse than debt'. It is not a result of recent developments, but of a long historical process which is worth recalling.

Where did it all start?

The Philippines was a direct colony of Spain, and then of the United States of America, for about four hundred years. In 1946, the Americans granted the country what is best described as 'flag independence', because in many ways, and especially in economic terms, that independence was hollow.

The post-liberation period saw a Philippine economy ravaged by World War II. Rehabilitation assistance from the United States became an overriding consideration for Filipino leaders. In exchange for such aid, they allowed 'parity rights' for American businesses, which meant the latter could operate public utilities and exploit the country's natural resources. Free-trade policies were also adopted, leading to the flooding of the domestic market by North American goods, and an acute balance-of-payments crisis by the late 1940s.

To ward off bankruptcy and prevent the growth of a communist-led rebellion, the government imposed import and exchange controls, with the approval of US President Truman. Twelve years of such controls made possible the rise of Filipino businesses, especially light industries to produce goods that would take the place of previously imported commodities. The entrepreneurs who set up these businesses were the force behind the 'Filipino First' policy adopted in 1958, which gave preferential treatment to Filipinos in the economic development of the country.

The foreign business community went on a counter-offensive. Pressures from foreign interests eventually succeeded in 1961 with the onset of the Macapagal administration, which immediately dropped the 'Filipino First' slogan, abolished import and foreign-exchange controls, and devalued the peso *vis à vis* the US dollar. Decontrol led to unlimited repatriation of profits by foreign corporations. Unrestricted imports resulted in an increasingly unfavourable balance of trade,[5] and subjected Filipino-manufactured goods to overwhelming competition. The depletion of foreign-exchange reserves led the Philippines into the 'debt trap', the cycle of permanent dependence on global financial institutions, principally the International Monetary Fund (IMF). Since the beginning of the Macapagal administration, the Philippines has had to adopt the prescriptions of the IMF on matters regarding economic policies and programmes in exchange for 'stabilisation loans'.[6]

IMF-imposed devaluation in the early 1960s had the most crippling effects on Filipino businesses, which had to pay almost double for every dollar's worth of capital goods they had to import. On the other hand, it was most advantageous to foreign investors, whose dollars could buy almost twice as much as they used to. Under these circumstances, it was very easy for North American corporations to take over struggling Filipino industries.

Policies favourable to foreign interests continued during the administration of President Ferdinand Marcos. In 1967, the Investment Incentives Act allowed even business enterprises not possessing the required proportion of Philippine ownership and control to operate in preferred, non-pioneer areas of investment under certain conditions. After the 1969 elections, characterised by massive electoral overspending which pushed the country to the verge of bankruptcy, the Philippine peso was again devalued against the US dollar, as a result of IMF pressure. The Philippine government had to bow to the pressure or accept an end to the aid and credit which it desperately needed. Devaluation was again a boon to foreign investors and exporters. The losers were the Filipino manufacturers, who had to bear higher costs of imports and repayments of foreign borrowings, as well as tighter credit restrictions. Many Filipino industries folded up or were taken over by foreign-owned competitors. The inflation resulting from devaluation also greatly reduced the real income of the Filipino working people.[7]

Foreign domination of the Philippine economy was considerably strengthened during the martial-law years (1972-1986). The country was placed even more firmly in the debt trap, with its foreign obligations estimated at $25-$30 billion. In securing those loans, it had to accede to the demands of its creditors, principally the World Bank and the IMF, together with 483 foreign commercial banks. Such demands involved the virtual surrender of the country's economic sovereignty. Transnational corporations (TNCs) increased their production of relatively inexpensive – and therefore competitive – products for the world market, using low-cost Filipino labour and raw materials.

The 53 per cent devaluation of the peso in 1983, which even the government-influenced media admitted to be an IMF imposition, ruined many Filipino businesses (now an 'endangered species'). It benefited only foreign firms whose dollars could facilitate their takeover of floundering enterprises, and dollar-earning export industries tied to the global market controlled by TNCs. The mass of Filipino consumers, already reeling from the soaring inflation triggered by the double devaluation, had to bear increased water and electricity rates and higher taxes and charges for government services, which again were World Bank-IMF recommendations.

The Philippine debt crisis became a full-blown one during the Marcos regime. In 1965, the beginning of the Marcos administration, the country's debt burden was a mere $599 million. By 1970, this had risen to $2.3 billion; by 1975 to $4.9 billion; by 1983 (the beginning of the end for the Marcos dictatorship as waves of protest followed the assassination of Benigno Aquino, Jr., the most prominent opposition leader), to $24.1 billion; and by February 1986 (when the Marcos regime collapsed and the administration of Corazon Aquino took over), to $26.3 billion.[8]

Two factors contributed to this increasing debt burden. One was the over-eagerness of the big North American, Japanese and European banks to lend billions of petrodollars to developing countries, including the Philippines, in the 1970s. The other was the borrowing spree which Marcos' allies engaged in, to finance business empires which piled up debts which were later passed on to the government to assume. These two factors aggravated the long-standing problem of balance of payment

John Clark/Oxfam

In the foreground: shanty houses; in the background: a grandiose legacy of the Marcos regime, poorly constructed and already crumbling.

deficits caused by trade deficits and profit remittances, which had to be financed by more and more foreign borrowings. It is noteworthy that during the entire post-war period, the Philippines enjoyed a trade surplus only three times (1963, 1966, and 1973).[9]

The profligacy of the Marcos family was legendary. Luxurious buildings and 'white elephants' abound to this day as testimonials to the First Lady's truly impressive 'edifice complex'. All this, plus the vast array of shoes, clothes, art works, and other worldly possessions now on display at Malacanang Palace, must have cost millions of dollars and brought pressure to bear on the foreign-exchange reserves.

The administration of President Cory Aquino, instead of making a clean break with the Marcos past, promised to pay the Marcos debts 'if only for honour'. Her administration also adopted the same economic policies so closely identified with IMF-World Bank prescriptions.

Who gains from the debt?

We can find the answers to this question by looking at who borrows, who lends, and where the borrowed money goes.

Using 1989 figures, we find that more than 80 per cent of the $28 billion debt was owed by the public sector, meaning the Central Bank, and government-owned or controlled corporations such as the Philippine

National Bank, the Development Bank of the Philippines, the National Power Corporation, etc. This means that ultimately, most of the debt will be paid by government from the national budget. Taxpayers will have to shell out more money, and people will have to forego much-needed social services. The other 20 per cent of the national debt was accounted for by the private sector, meaning the large banks, manufacturers and traders, many of which are global or transnational corporations.

More than half of the debt was owed to commercial banks, which means that the country was hostage to fluctuating interest rates in the international financial market. Because a one per cent increase in interest rates results in a $130 million rise in interest payments, an additional $260 million had to be released in 1988 because of the two per cent increase in interest rates. Almost one quarter of the debt was owed to the governments of countries like the United States and Japan, while almost one fifth was owed to multilateral institutions such as the World Bank, the International Monetary Fund, and the Asian Development Bank.[10]

The creditors benefit from the debt by profiting from interest payments. They make sure that old debts are paid through new debts, so nobody loses money through debtor default. (From 1972-1983, an average of 53.5 per cent of new borrowings went on repayments.[11]) In fact, there seems to be a shift from direct investments to interest payments as the main source of extracting surplus from the developing countries.

In exchange for new loans, multilateral financial institutions such as the IMF and World Bank, and various consultative groups of creditor banks and countries, are also able to influence governments to implement policies favourable to them. These policies can be collectively described as 'structural adjustment', which according to the World Bank includes:

> ... a range of measures intended to reduce internal and external deficits, increase efficiency in the economy, and reduce government expenditure. Typically, they would include (1) changing the exchange rate to reflect more closely the true value of the currency ... (2) reducing government payrolls; (3) selling to private interests or dismantling government-owned enterprises; (4) raising agricultural prices closer to world market levels ... and (5) reducing subsidies both on consumption items, including food, and to producers.[12]

In the Philippine experience, creditor-imposed policies also include the liberalising of controls on imports, new taxes, higher public utility rates, wage freezes, credit squeezes, and efforts to increase foreign-exchange earnings, in particular through the expansion of exports. As summarised by one source, the principle of the conditions imposed by the International Monetary Fund is that 'the debtor country must tighten its belt so it would spend less and earn foreign exchange'.[13]

All this favours foreign creditors in particular and foreign business in general in a number of ways. Deregulation and import liberalisation leave the market wide open for penetration and inundation by foreign products. Imported apples, for example, are now on sale in most shopping areas. They are cheaper than local mangoes, which have become scarce. Privatisation drives government out of the scene, leaving the field to global concerns which are in the best position to take over even the most lucrative public corporations. Devaluation and wage freezes make Filipino labour even cheaper than before, and render transnational exports even more competitive in the global market.

No wonder foreign investors are having a heyday, at the expense of the Filipino people. The Freedom From Debt Coalition cites Central Bank data which show that from 1970-1987, more dollars were pumped out of the country in the form of profit remittances, royalties, fees, etc. than the dollars that came in as investments. In-flow totalled $2.557 billion, versus an out-flow of $3.734, resulting in a net out-flow of $1.177 billion.[14]

The Filipino elite also benefited from the debt. During the Marcos regime, there were claims that negotiators and their staff benefited from payments to make 'feasibility studies' (often with the advice of expensive foreign consultants) and to go on expensive trips abroad.

The bureaucracies and officialdom of corporate borrowers also benefited, accused by one observer in 1984 of building 'five-star staff houses, rest houses, and sports complexes all over the country; [they] acquire helicopters and charter private planes; and raise salaries to astro-nomical levels ...'.[15]

'Lobbyists', 'high-level fixers', and businessmen-supporters of the political elite (commonly known in the Philippines as 'cronies') benefited as they 'negotiated' with lending institutions and 'liaised' with suppliers and contractors in return for a share of the total loan. The most notorious case involving bribery was that of the Bataan nuclear power plant, where evidence compiled by a member institution of the Freedom From Debt Coalition suggests that a Marcos 'crony' (Herminio Disini) received a five per cent commission from the US corporation Westinghouse in exchange for clinching the deal. Estimates of this commission range from $55 million to $80 million.[16]

Private corporations owned by 'cronies' also benefited as they incurred loans they did not deserve, and later passed on the loans for government to assume. During the Marcos period, such 'crony corporations' had loan exposures in the hundreds of millions of dollars.[17]

It is also quite likely that corrupt Filipino officials, like their counterparts elsewhere in the Third World, siphoned out money to foreign banks, which re-lent the money to the country, only to be siphoned out again by the local elite.

The price of honour

Central Bank figures show that for 1989, the debt-service burden reached $3.116 billion, $2.217 billion for interest and $899 million for principal.[18] The World Bank estimated that total debt service for the years 1989 and 1990 would reach $7.3 billion.[19]

The Aquino administration, as mentioned earlier, has pledged to honour all the debts accumulated by the country. It has chosen a conciliatory, non-confrontational stance towards foreign creditors, preferring to renegotiate for better terms of repayment and also for more borrowings to repay old loans. It offers attractive options like debt-for-equity swaps, by which foreigners buying debt papers in dollars can convert them into pesos and buy into Filipino corporations at a huge discount.

Debt service as a percentage of the national budget rose from 24.5 per cent in 1986, the year the Aquino administration took over, to 44 per cent in 1989. Ironically, the government still follows a decree left over from the Marcos era, stipulating that national funds be automatically provided for debt service without having to be approved by the legislature. In so doing, the Aquino administration violates the 1987 Constitution that it brought into being, which specifies that Congress is the only entity which can make appropriations.

Debt negotiations have always been the responsibility of the Central Bank and the Department of Finance. The terms of such negotiations have always been shrouded in secrecy; the people who would be most affected by the outcome have always been excluded from influencing the negotiating strategy.

Invariably, the government position is circumscribed by the condition-alities imposed by creditors, principally the IMF, within the framework of 'adjustment'. Together with the stick, there is always a carrot: in the

Philippine case, the promise of 'new money' and more 'aid' in the form of such initiatives as the Philippine Aid Plan (which is described later in this chapter).

The 'Letter of Intent'

The 'Letter of Intent' (LoI), which contains a Memorandum of Economic Policy from the Philippines to the IMF, was formulated by a small group of officials with guidance from IMF officials. Issued in March 1989, it prescribes economic targets for 1989-1992, on the basis of which the government secured a new $1.3 billion loan, $1.1 billion of which will be used to repay old loans. As one source exclaimed, 'We borrow again in order to pay back what we borrowed before!'[20]

As expected, the LoI prescribed the usual adjustment formula, which consists principally of austerity measures so that the government can pay back its debt. These measures include :

- increasing taxes;
- transferring the debt of private corporations to the national government (which means that ordinary citizens will ultimately pay for it in terms of higher taxes or foregone services);
- the removal of government subsidy for and control over the price of rice;
- increasing charges exacted by public utility corporations;
- limiting government expenditure on its own employees.

These measures are fundamentally opposed to the interests and welfare of the poor, as we shall see in the next chapter.

Solita Collas-Monsod, former Economic Planning Secretary who left the government after she had unsuccessfully opposed IMF conditionalities, shed light in subsequent papers and interviews on why the government rushed into such an onerous commitment. She claimed that during her time, 'The IMF framework was unacceptable to the Philippine authorities.'[21] Its growth targets were too low, and would result in 'decreases in what were considered vital infrastructure and current expenditures'. Negotiations with the IMF were suspended but were later revived, only to culminate in the LoI.

According to Solita Monsod, the proponents of the LoI justified its hasty issue by citing Philippine arrears which might lead to the suspension of loan disbursements. They also emphasised the need to make progress towards the realisation of the Philippine Aid Plan.

The Philippine Aid Plan

The Philippine Aid Plan (PAP) is supposed to be a mechanism by which developed countries, particularly the United States and Japan, can provide economic assistance to the Philippines. Its history is linked to the negotiations on the US military bases in the country, as the Washington administration, with its huge budgetary and trade deficits, tries to share the burden of retaining these bases with others in lieu of direct compensation or rental.[22]

The PAP is based on a comprehensive country programme which contains virtually the policies and prescriptions of the World Bank and the IMF. This programme, entitled 'The Philippine Agenda for Sustained Growth and Development', served as the basis for discussion during the pledging session for the PAP which took place in Tokyo in July 1989; this session supposedly resulted in a total of $3.5 billion in grants and loans for 1989. However, Solita Monsod, former Secretary for Economic Planning, says that new pledges amount only to $251.3 million for 1989, and $986 million for 1989-1992.[23] In brief, the PAP could never be the solution to the debt problem of the Philippines.

3

What the debt means to the poor

When we talk about the poor, we are talking about at least half of the Filipino population of 62 million people. According to official data, the incidence of poverty in the population in 1988 was 49.5 per cent. This figure is based on a poverty threshold of P2,709 (£56.43), defined as the 'minimum amount of monthly income that a family of six members need to meet its nutritional requirements and other basic needs'.[1]

Government data, however, contrast sharply with unofficial sources. Many economists in the same period counted 70 per cent of the population as living in absolute poverty, meaning that they 'cannot buy for their families recommended nutrient requirements, cannot permit two changes of garments, cannot permit Grade 6 schooling for the children, cannot cover minimal costs of medical care and cannot pay for fuel and rent'.[2]

It is enough to say at this point that too many of the people are poor. Among them are farmers (upland and lowland), agricultural workers, fisherfolk, and the low-paid and marginalised sectors in the urban areas who are collectively known as the 'urban poor'. In general, there have always been more poor people in the rural areas than in the urban areas. In general, too, there are more women and female-headed households among the poor, because of their low status in society, and the commonly low remuneration for women's work.

One reason why there are so many poor Filipinos is that the rich monopolise so much of the wealth and income. The 1988 World Development Report shows that the Philippines 'has one of the most inequitable distributions of income in Asia compared to India, Indonesia, Sri Lanka, and Bangladesh'. The basis for such a conclusion is that 'The percentage share of Philippine household income for the bottom 20 per cent was pegged at 5.2 per cent in 1985', while 'the highest 10 per cent of households in the Philippines accounted for a hefty 36.4 per cent share'.[3] Figures for 1988 were about the same.

The UNICEF study on the Philippines (included in the book *Adjustment with a Human Face*) says that 'low-income families are characterized by (a) lack of productive assets or control over such assets; (b) limited use of modern technology in their production activities; (c) limited

Belinda Coote/Oxfam

Urban poverty: Barrio Simento, Davao City.

access to basic economic and social services; and (d) limited human capital'.[4]

This same study revealed some of the causes and the dynamics of poverty. Referring to the 'lack of resource base and asset control', it noted primarily the highly distorted distribution of land: fifty-two per cent of low-income families did not own the land they were cultivating, and 35 per cent cultivated farms smaller than a hectare.

Most low-income families use traditional subsistence methods of agriculture, partly because modern technology is too expensive for them. Thus 'only one-fifth have irrigated land, a little more than one-third use pesticides and fertilizers, less than a quarter use high-yielding varieties, and less than a third practise interplanting or double cropping'.

'Limited human capital', according to the UNICEF study, is manifested in lower levels of literacy and education among low-income families. The study cites the 1983 Integrated Survey of Households which shows that of those over 15 years of age among low-income families, '10 per cent did not go to school, 37 per cent had some elementary schooling, 26 per cent completed elementary schooling, and 13 per cent had attended high school'.[5] If it takes at least seven years of schooling to ensure functional literacy, then about three-quarters of the poor who did not complete the six-year elementary schooling may not really be able to read and write.

In more direct terms, how then does the debt affect the poor? First, because of the huge amount that government has to allocate for debt servicing, very little is left to provide for the needs of the poor. Working on the 1989 budget figures (43.9 per cent for debt service versus 38.7 per cent for economic and social services), one source claims 'each family loses P10,000 (about £208) worth of government services simply because of the foreign debt'.[6]

The poor use government schools and government hospitals, if they can, because they cannot afford to pay fees for private educational and medical services. In 1989, the Department of Education, Culture and Sports received only P24.675 billion (£514 million), and the Department of Health only P7.024 billion (£146 million) compared to P97.712 billion (£2.03 billion) spent on debt service.[7]

The problem, however, does not end here. Out of the allocated sums for social services, the amount that is actually spent on the poor (conservatively estimated at 50 per cent of the population), after subtracting the salaries of government personnel, as well as maintenance and other operating expenses, is only P880 per capita or P5,280 (£110) per family.[8]

This figure should be compared with what the government takes from the poor in the form of taxes (P8,000 per family),[9] much of which is exacted by government in response to debt-related financial difficulties. The system of taxation is regressive, which means that indirect taxes on goods and services (of which the poor consume more) account for a greater percentage of total taxes than taxes on income and property. The poor pay taxes every time they take a bus ride, every time they use gas to cook a meal, and every time they see a movie.

These taxes are in compliance with the provisions of the 1989 Letter of Intent (LoI), which endorses the government's economic policies in response to conditions imposed by the IMF. The LoI seeks to raise revenue collection by P25.9 billion, not only through new taxes but also by increasing charges for services provided by government corporations, which means higher electricity, water and port rates, which the poor also pay for.

L Freeby/Oxfam

Family shoe-repair stall in Manila.

The poor are affected by IMF-imposed policies in other ways, too. The removal of government subsidy on and control over the price of rice has already resulted in a steep price rise. Filipino families who rely on rice to provide the bulk of their meagre diet now face the prospect of increasing hunger. The rapid devaluation of the peso against the US dollar means a drastic rise in the prices of imports, primarily oil, industrial raw materials, and equipment. This drives up the cost of transportation and basic goods.

With devaluation and the resultant inflation, the purchasing power of the poor is fast decreasing. Whatever increase in pay or income they manage to win through concerted effort is seldom sufficient even to regain what they have lost. Workers who are unorganised, unheard, and invisible, many of them women and children, have to make do with stagnant earnings while prices escalate.

Out of desperation, many Filipinos, conservatively estimated at one and a half million, now work overseas, where they can earn dollar incomes many times the maximum they could get were they to remain at home. With the estimated $2.5 billion they remit annually, they are, in a very real sense, the ones paying for the country's debt.

4

Health: a life or debt question

According to a leading national newspaper, not repaying the debt could save the life of one Filipino child every hour. This could be achieved by limiting the debt service to 20 per cent of export earnings, and allotting health its rightful share from the savings realised in the national budget.[1] This is indeed an emotionally powerful argument for a ceiling on debt servicing. But the Philippine Congress has not approved a bill seeking to limit debt service, despite strenuous lobbying efforts by the Freedom From Debt Coalition and other concerned groups.

Recent years have seen an inverse relationship between debt service and health spending in total national government expenditures. As debt service sharply increased (from 6.4 per cent in 1965-72, to 17.1 per cent in 1980-85, and finally to 42 per cent in 1986-89), health expenditure steadily declined (from 5.2 per cent in 1965-72 to 3.2 per cent in 1986-89).[2] Health was allocated 3.3 per cent in the 1990 budget, compared with the 37 per cent allocated to debt service. On a per capita basis, this budget for health is P120 (£2.50) for the year, or 30 centavos per day.[3]

As a result of the IMF conditions acknowledged in the Letter of Intent, the Department of Health even expects a sizeable reduction in its beneficiaries. This reduction means 'leaving 399,120 children denied milk and vitamins, 27,565 lepers deprived of treatment, 103,262 TB [tuberculosis] patients untreated, and 16,100 schistosomiasis cases denied medicines'.[4]

Health Secretary Alfredo Bengzon is himself quite candid about the budgetary limitations to health care. For example, when he was asked (in 1989) how much the Department of Health needed in order to provide basic medicines for fever, diarrhoea and other ordinary ailments, he estimated 900 million to one billion pesos. But the figure finally allocated in the budget was P300 million (£6.25 million).[5]

Government spending accounts for only 25 per cent of total health expenditures in the country.[6] Most of the hospitals are privately owned and cater to the relatively better off in the urban areas. Of the public hospitals, some 80 per cent are considered substandard by health experts and workers.

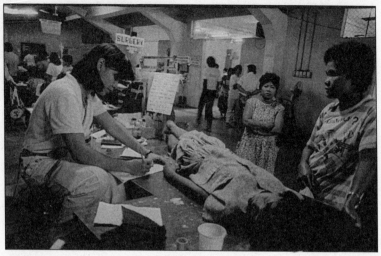

Gil Nartea

Government hospitals are over-crowded, under-staffed, and poorly equipped.

The Alliance of Health Workers provides some first-hand observations. It claims that almost all government hospitals are overcrowded because most people, even the middle class, can no longer afford the services of private hospitals. During peak periods, there are two to three patients in one bed in the paediatrics and the obstetrics/gynaecological sections. There are sometimes four in a crib. In the provincial hospitals, wooden beds are added to the regular beds; sometimes, the patients bring their own. Even corridors are full of patients in bed. The overcrowding is aggravated by the increasing shortage of health personnel, especially of nurses. The average ratio of nurses to patients in government hospitals is 1:60, and in the worst cases it can go as high as 1:120.

Because every government hospital has a set budget, which is woefully inadequate, medicines, supplies and services which are supposed to be given free of charge now have to be paid for even before the patient receives treatment. Examples are drug samples, bandages, sutures, plaster, intravenous fluid, steam inhalation and sponge baths. Funds which used to be enough for one quarter are now used up in three weeks, because budgetary allocations do not change despite inflation. Money which could buy five rolls for making cotton balls years ago may buy only one roll now. And there are even more patients than before.

The plight of the health workers

With the monthly minimum wage for workers in the public sector pegged at P2,000 (about £41) – when the cost of living for a family of five totals P6,600 (about £137) a month – many health workers, desperate and demoralised, are opting out by going abroad. Many others have become vendors on the side, selling such items as food, clothes, and cosmetics. Estimates of the number of Filipino physicians trained in the Philippines who have left for employment overseas range from nearly half to more than two-thirds.[7]

Roughly six out of ten Filipinos live and die without seeing a doctor. The rural areas, where 60 per cent of the population live, are notoriously underserved. There are more than 40,000 villages, but only 1,155 rural health officers. A majority of the doctors work in the cities, primarily in Metro Manila, where almost half of all hospital beds are concentrated.

Nationally, there is one doctor for every 3,000 Filipinos, way below the global standard of 1:1000.[8] Fewer than a third of registered physicians work in the government health service. Because salaries are so low, the vacancy rate in government health posts is as high as 15 per cent for physicians, and 11 per cent for nurses. Dr Orville Solon, a health economist connected with the University of the Philippines, points out the danger that 'cheap doctors' of uncertain qualification are being taken in; there is no way to monitor their performance and possible malpractice, because monitoring costs money.[9]

In the period 1985-87, a total of 65,940 Filipino nurses were deployed abroad.[10] A World Health Organization study in 1980 cited the Philippines as the biggest supplier of nurses to other countries. Then, there were 13,500 Filipino nurses abroad, or about 88 per cent of all those trained in the Philippines. The reason for the continuing exodus is easy to understand. The minimum monthly salary for a nurse in the Philippines is P3,102 (less than $150). The going rate in the Middle East is $600 per month, and in the United States it is $2,000-3,000.

The brain drain, or 'reverse transfer of technology', deprives the nation not only of the services of doctors and nurses but also of the resources that were devoted to their training. Government policy is to encourage this export of labour. Medical and nursing schools, responding to the higher demand for their graduates abroad, continue to gear the training they offer to Western practice.

The deadliest plague: poverty

While the health care system deteriorates, the people fall victim to disease and neglect. Most are already vulnerable because of their poverty.

Only 15 per cent of the population have a sanitary sewerage system, and about 40 per cent have no access to potable water – this while at least 31 out of 100,000 Filipinos die of water-borne and water-connected diseases every year.[11] Most people cannot afford such 'modern' installations and the government, desperate for funds, cannot provide them.

Food is getting scarcer and more expensive. A full 70 per cent of the population is said to be malnourished, 22 per cent to a serious degree. Food shortage is evident in the daily calorie availability of 2214 per capita (compared to the 2500 standard set by the World Health Organization) and in the daily protein availability of 60 grammes per capita (compared to the 70-gramme standard).[12]

Poor nutrition, bad housing, and insanitary conditions for the poor make them susceptible to the diseases of poverty, particularly tuberculosis, which, according to Health Minister Alfredo R.A. Bengzon, afflicted 18 million Filipinos in 1986.[13] TB is the fourth highest cause of mortality; the first is pneumonia. Other leading causes of death – diarrhoea, measles, and nutritional deficiencies – are preventable and would have been easy to control, if only the health care system were more effective.

Children and women are especially vulnerable. About 25 per cent of Filipinos, mostly infants and pregnant and lactating mothers, are afflicted by anaemia. The current infant mortality rate (IMR) is placed at 56.8 per 1000 live births. (The IMR rose from 56.9 in 1980 to 62.8 per 1,000 in 1984, which 'was not unexpected, given the increased economic difficulties and cutbacks in government health expenditures and other social services that characterized this period' – also a period of intense debt crisis.[14]) If the babies survive, many fall victim to malnutrition, said to afflict 70 to 80 per cent of all children below the age of six. Mental retardation is often the fate of the severely malnourished.

Maternal mortality rate, on the other hand, is almost one (0.9) per 1,000 live births, meaning that five Filipino mothers a day, or about 2,000 a year, die from pregnancy-related causes. A Filipino pregnant woman risks death a hundred times more than her counterpart in a developed country. Causes of maternal mortality – haemorrhage, hypertension and other complications (including infection) – are preventable if prospective mothers are well-fed and have good prenatal care.[15] Haemorrhage is frequently caused by anaemia, which afflicts 48.7 per cent of pregnant women.[16] The vulnerability of women is heightened by the estimated

Belinda Coote/Oxfam

Negros: A 31 year-old sugar worker, suffering from tuberculosis for ten years without treatment, mounts his own protest to demand access to a properly equipped clinic with a doctor.

number of induced abortions performed yearly – 155,000-750,000 – under illegal conditions.[17] The risk of dying from illegal abortion is 1,000 to 2,000 times higher than from legal abortion.

Children of the poor, like their mothers, cannot be given as much attention as they need. Government-run day-care centres, which number only 13,003, double as supplementary feeding stations for malnourished children. They provide services for only two to three hours a day on average. This means that children of working mothers cannot be looked after by the centres for the whole time that their mothers are at work.

In short, debt keeps people in a vicious cycle of poverty and ill health, and renders government services helpless to do anything about it.

Campaigning for 'sane' drugs

SANE is the acronym that the Health Action Information Network (HAIN) has coined to popularise rational drug use among the people. It stands for Safe, Affordable, Needed, and Effective, to contrast with the dangerous, expensive, unnecessary and impotent medicines which still command a large share of the market dominated by transnational drug companies based mainly in the United States and Western Europe.

According to Michael L. Tan of HAIN, 'We estimate that Filipinos spend one billion pesos a year on cough and cold remedies which are completely useless actually.'[18] Needless to say, if people can be persuaded to buy and use only SANE drugs, a lot of money can be saved for other needs. More dollars can be conserved, rather than spent on importing the raw materials for unnecessary medicines, thus easing the pressure on scarce supplies of foreign exchange. On the part of government, reducing purchases to a list of essential drugs can help to maximise already scarce financial resources.

Michael Tan is the first to admit that the SANE campaign cannot hope to close the ever-widening gap between what is needed and what is available, given the budgetary cuts suffered as a consequence of IMF conditionalities. 'The budget of the Department of Health has already been slashed by five per cent by the House of Representatives. Given 15 per cent inflation, it is really 20 per cent lower,' he reports.

The problem is magnified by the fact that the Department of Health has a budget of only P400 million (around £8 million) for medicines, when DoH officials themselves admit that if they were to meet the needs of the poor, they would need P10 billion (around £208 million).

Nevertheless, HAIN is still pursuing its SANE campaign, conscious of the need to promote rational drug use within the broader goal of eventually fostering self-sufficiency in the currently import-dependent and foreign-controlled drug industry. OXFAM supports its efforts by giving full financial support for a pharmaceuticals coordinator and a researcher, and partial support for three other members of the HAIN staff. In addition, OXFAM funds a regular HAIN publication called *Drug Monitor*, as well as other educational materials.

Michael Tan admits the limitations of relying on printed materials. As he says, 'Let's face it – the Philippines is not a reading public.' Thus, HAIN places more emphasis on symposia, workshops and other face-to-face encounters where issues are explained directly and with a lot of visual aids. 'The participatory element is assured when we require the participants to do a little survey on the most popular drugs in their community or in their particular organisation,' Michael explains. 'You'd be amazed at the amount of unnecessary spending going on. All kinds of useless drugs are being bought even by progressive non-governmental organisations, causing needless expenditures that can be put to better use.'

'But the bigger problem which we are only now beginning to address is the fact that the people still cannot afford the medicines they need,' Michael emphasises. 'And given the debt crisis which affects government spending, too, their only possible source of affordable drugs is also drying up.'

So, in the interests of promoting rational drug use, the HAIN group is also supporting the Generics Act. With the use of generic drug names, people are now able to choose the most inexpensive drug from the many in the market which have the same chemical effectiveness but bear different brand names. HAIN is conscious of the need to develop the technological base for a self-sufficient drug industry. Michael Tan even entertains the idea of going into manufacturing. But the first stage of entering the business, he feels, should be mass procurement or wholesaling.

HAIN came into being in 1985. In its short span of life, the group has published valuable research which has helped to shape and maintain the national drug policy.

5

Education: down from number one

'Make education number one.' This is the rallying cry of Filipino teachers as they continue to protest against conditions imposed on the economy by the International Monetary Fund and campaign for a higher allocation for education in the national budget. In this they are actually adhering to the spirit and letter of the fundamental law of the land.

The 1987 Constitution of the Republic of the Philippines states in Article XIV, Section 5. (5): 'The State shall assign the highest budgetary priority to education and ensure that teaching will attract and retain its rightful share of the best available talents through adequate remuneration and other means of job satisfaction and fulfillment.' This constitutional provision reflects the Filipino people's traditionally high regard for education as a means for personal as well as national development. In fact, in many of the post-war years, education actually took the biggest slice of the national budget.

But in 1990 debt-service allocation ate up P86.8 billion, or 37 per cent of the national budget, in contrast to education's P33.2 billion, or 14 per cent. The low budget for education means less money for teachers' salaries, school facilities, supplies and textbooks, and generally a deterioration in the quality of instruction. Free secondary education, also provided for by the 1987 Constitution, will be even more difficult to sustain.

The shortfalls are striking. When, in 1989, the Department of Education, Culture and Sports (DECS) was asked how many more classrooms were needed for inclusion in the budget, DECS said 18,000. But only 8,000 could be provided. Thus, teachers even in Quezon City, Metro Manila can be seen holding classes under mango trees and in double shifts, morning and afternoon.[1]

Another effect of the financial crisis is overcrowding. According to Benjamin Balbuena, a teacher at the F.G. Calderon Integrated School and vice-president of the Manila Public School Teachers' Association, class size can go up to 60 students from the usual 40 students. This, he says, is no longer conducive to learning. He cites as proof the sudden drop from 50 to 25 per cent in the number of students who passed the National College Entrance Examination (NCEE) in 1990. 'This,' he insists, 'is not an isolated case. What is true in our school is also true in other schools in Manila.'[2]

The lack of equipment and teaching aids has reached the level of absurdity. According to Mr Balbuena, the institution where he teaches is already called the 'school of assumption': in the science class, the teacher tells the students, 'Let us assume that this is a microscope', because there is no microscope; in his case as an electronics instructor, Balbuena repeats the same formula: 'Let us assume that this is a multi-tester', because there is no multi-tester. The school does not even have hammers or pliers. He tried requisitioning for such essential equipment, but it is always 'subject to the availability of funds', and the final decision, taken several rungs up the educational bureaucracy, is: 'no funds available'.

Educational standards suffer. Many high schools no longer offer mathematics and basic sciences because of lack of resources, says Ed Escultura, professor of mathematics in the University of the Philippines.[3] Desperate school officials and teachers are often reduced to soliciting donations and other fund-raising activities. Parents and students often end up donating laboratory equipment and other school needs which otherwise cannot be obtained. In government high schools, where students are supposed to be charged only a token sum of P42.50 (because secondary education is free according to law), fees over and above this legal limit are often collected, according to Benjamin Balbuena. Schools are passing on the financial burden to students because the government can no longer shoulder it.

But perhaps the most worrying trend is the worsening lack of teachers, and the consequent overloading of those who remain in the service. DECS statistics showed that at least 44,207 teachers more were needed for government elementary and high schools for the school year 1989-90. This number included the backlog of unoccupied positions numbering 13,305 from the previous school year. The DECS explains this shortfall first in terms of unattractive salary rates, and then in terms of the lucrative rewards from overseas employment: many teachers would rather work as domestic help or chambermaids abroad, than live a life of deprivation and sacrifice at home.[4]

What happens to those who choose to serve and suffer? They suffer even more. In places like Cebu, where no new teaching positions can be created due to DECS' budgetary constraints, acting provincial school superintendent Marcelo Bacalso says teachers already in the service will be asked to handle bigger classes of 60 to 70 students each.[5]

Another measure is to increase the teaching load or double the number of classes previously handled by teachers. Because the hiring of substitute teachers is no longer allowed, again due to cost-cutting, teachers in active service have to take on the load of their colleagues who go on leave.

Teachers speak out

Teachers who remain in the service are overworked (because they have to teach more classes and more students per class) and underpaid: the minimum salary is P3,102 (£64.62), which is equivalent to only P648.93 (£13.51) by 1978 standards. Merlinda Anonuevo, an English teacher at the M. Hizon Elementary School in Tondo, Manila, asks 'How can you maintain your dignity if all you can afford for housing is a one-room affair for P800 where you are forced to stay with your husband and five children? How can you send your children to college, when the tuition fees are going up all the time? No wonder so many teachers become insurance or real estate agents, or start selling jewellery and sweets, or give up teaching altogether to be domestic helpers abroad.'[6]

Vangie Ricasio, a high school teacher in F.G. Calderon Integrated School, lives as a squatter on a squalid government lot. She describes the fate of a colleague to show how desperate the situation can become.[7] This colleague – her name was Mrs Remy Apora – was murdered by an unidentified assailant, together with her adopted daughter and son, inside their shanty. The place was so small, it could accommodate only a double bed, a rusty refrigerator, a stove and a few other belongings. According to neighbours, they did not realise that Mrs Apora was a teacher from the way she looked and lived. Her husband was in Saudi Arabia, where he was maltreated by his employer and was unable to send money regularly. She was always in debt, and more so lately when she was trying to produce P30,000 to prevent a piece of land she was paying for from being repossessed due to arrears which had piled up. Her only possible sources were her co-teachers but they too, were hard up. Their common plight as teachers became the focus of protest rallies, which Mrs Apora attended with her small children in tow – until they were murdered.

Merlinda Anonuevo and Vangie Ricasio are just two out of thousands of teachers who are already used to walkouts, marches and other street actions to press for higher salaries.[8] The minimum salary of P3,102 is a result of their struggle, although it still falls far short of their target of P4,500.

At first, the demands of the teachers' associations were purely economic, but recently their concerns have reached the political plane,

Gil Nartea

Teachers' hunger strike, November 1990.

and are more readily connected to wider issues like the foreign debt. Teachers like Merlinda and Vangie support moves to staunch the debt haemorrhage. 'We are for limiting debt service to 15 per cent of export earnings,' they comment. 'We hope that the money thus released from debt payments can go to education, health and other social services.'

6

Debt, labour, and employment

In October 1989 official figures on unemployment conservatively estimated the proportion of jobless people at 8.4 per cent of the estimated 23.8 million total labour force, and estimated the rate of underemployment at 32.4 per cent of the estimated 21.8 million actually in employment.[1] These figures mean there are at least two million Filipinos openly unemployed, and more than seven million have no full-time jobs, or are working fewer than 40 hours a week. These statistics do not reflect the 'invisibly underemployed': those who have 'full-time' jobs and are still seeking additional work because their present occupations give them very limited returns. Moreover, some of the unemployed may not have been reflected in the statistics, because the labour force participation rate is only 64.6 out of every 100 people. This means that some of the unemployed may have been lumped together with those classified 'not in the labour force', mostly women who are 'housewives' (who number 13 million out of the 36.9 million population of working age).

Debt creates unemployment

The debt problem contributes to unemployment directly by preventing the government from performing to the optimum one of its vital functions: that of a creator of jobs and a pump primer of the economy whenever the latter is weakening or stagnant. The national debt service would be equivalent to paying three million people a minimum wage of P2,500 per month (thereby wiping out the official unemployment figure of two million), or it could be invested in job-creation schemes such as improving infrastructure, building schools and hospitals, and accelerating agrarian reform.

To create jobs, the Philippines needs capital. Hence the endless campaign of the government to attract foreign investment. And yet, because of the debt problem, the Philippines is now a major exporter of capital. An official source claims that in the period 1986-88, the country in effect exported $6.1 billion to outside creditors in the form of interest payments.[2]

In addition, certain conditionalities imposed by the IMF and World Bank in exchange for new loans or loan agreements directly aggravate the problem of unemployment. This is especially true in the case of IMF austerity measures such as new taxes, which reduce the purchasing power of the population and the overall demand for production. Restrictive monetary targets drive interest rates up and discourage new investments. And reduced government spending on social services and infrastructure depresses national consumption. For instance, the economy slowed down in the first half of 1990, and not necessarily because of the after-effects of a coup attempt against the Aquino administration in December 1989. As pointed out by the Director-General of the National Economic and Development Authority, Cayetano Paderanga, the slowdown was due more to economic factors such as the rise of interest rates to over 20 per cent, as a result of the government's compliance with the IMF's monetary and deficit targets.[3]

The underground economy

In the 1960s and 1970s, industry was contributing 15-16 per cent of total employment, with manufacturing accounting for 10-11 per cent. However, in the 1980s, when the debt crisis worsened, industrial employment went down to 13-14 per cent of total employment; manufacturing decreased to 9-10 per cent, a clear sign of de-industrialisation.[4]

The decline, instead of the expected advance, of industrial employment led to increased employment in the service sector and the so-called underground or 'black' economy, where jobs are precarious and labour standards mandated by law are rarely respected. The growth of the underground economy has been hailed, even romanticised, by some economists as a reflection of the entrepreneurial talents of the people. The truth is that its growth is more of a forced response by many people, especially those laid off or those earning very little from their present jobs, to the crisis. Although some talents do stand out, for most people employment in the informal sector is merely a coping or survival mechanism.

The most vivid and tragic proof that the growth of the underground economy is indeed a survival response is the high incidence of child labour and prostitution in the country. The Bureau of Women and Young Workers estimates the total number of child workers at somewhere between five and seven million.[5] Children from five to 14 years old are forced to work because of extreme poverty. They accept all kinds of odd jobs, some of which are physically very hazardous. A number even sell their bodies to paedophiles from the West. As to prostitution, it is already an established fact that Manila is now one of the 'flesh capitals' of Asia.

Robert Gumpert/Oxfam

On the waterfront in Manila: children filling sacks with cement sand, to sell on building sites for a few pesos.

The total number of prostitutes in the country may be anything from 300,000 to one million.

The general weakness of the economy can also be seen in the increasing number of workers who are only casually employed. Subcontracting of jobs to small shops and even home-based workers is now an established pattern in industries making garments, toys, parts, shoes, leatherware, and furniture, and other light and labour-intensive industries, especially those oriented to the export market. This type of employment consigns the workers to piece-rate levels and allows the employers to save on factory overhead costs. With the enactment of the Law of Twenty, which gives fiscal incentives to firms with fewer than 20 employees, job subcontracting is likely to spread even further.

Parallel with the growth of job subcontracting is the rise in the hiring by employers of the so-called 'agency workers', or workers who are technically on the payroll of job-placement agencies and yet are under the supervision of the final employers. Employers resort to this arrangement because they are able to keep their workers perpetually 'casual', thus avoiding the need to pay for benefits enjoyed by regular workers, especially the unionised ones.[6]

Attacks on the trade unions

The development strategy inspired by the IMF and World Bank is inherently anti-union. This is so because the maintenance of a pool of cheap, productive and docile labour is necessary for the strategy to work. The strategy relies on the cheapness of Philippine labour as the country's 'comparative advantage' in the world market; hence, the production of labour-based manufactures for export. This is the reason why President Marcos, using martial law powers, tried to control organised labour and curb some of the rights of workers, especially their rights to organise and engage in concerted activities such as peaceful assembly, picketing and strikes. Some of the repressive laws enacted during the Marcos administration are still in force today. One example is the controversial 'free ingress and egress' provision of the Labour Code, which allows management representatives and materials free movement into and out of company premises, thereby undermining the effectiveness of many strikes. In effect, these labour-control measures enforced by the government decrease the bargaining power of the workers, whose position is already weakened by the existence of massive unemployment and underemployment arising from the limited expansion of the economy.

The weakening of the workers' bargaining power is best seen in the steady decline of real wages throughout the 1970s and 1980s, made possible by runaway inflation and limited wage adjustments granted by both the Marcos and Aquino administrations. The P106 daily minimum wage is about half the P195-P210 (£4.06-£4.37) level estimated to ensure a decent life for workers' households.[7]

The crisis of the economy has generally weakened organised labour, especially with the efforts of employers to resort increasingly to the employment of casual labour through the subcontracting of jobs and services.

Debt and the overseas contract workers

Finally, it should be pointed out that workers are not only the victims but also the real payers of the debt – through the taxes (mainly indirect) they contribute, through the export industries they work in to generate more dollars for the country, and through the remittances they send home as Filipino overseas contract workers.

Because of the job shortage and meagre incomes in the Philippines, many workers are obliged to go abroad and endure long and lonely separations from their families, just to be able to support their dependants. In the early 1970s, the Marcos administration encouraged the export of labour as a 'temporary' measure to help solve the problem of unemployment and underemployment. With the failure of the economy to take off, the export of labour has not only become permanent, but has also become the country's leading export industry. The Philippine Overseas Employment Administration (POEA) is now processing close to half a million contract workers a year. There are now more than two million land-based and sea-based Filipino contract workers all over the world, performing varied jobs, from entertainment to hospital management. Roughly, at least one-fifth of the population of 62 million are directly dependent on their remittances. Overseas contract employment, in effect, is the safety valve of the economy.

Filipino migrant workers are also the leading dollar earners. Close to a billion dollars a year are remitted by contract workers through the formal banking system. However, officials estimate that remittances sent through informal channels are higher than those going through the banking system. Hence the efforts of the Central Bank to catch all remittances through the banking system in order to enlarge its dollar holdings, which are vital to debt management.

Rosalinda Pineda-Ofreneo

Desa Canoy: mother, trade unionist, and sander in the rattan furniture industry.

Desa Canoy: homeworker, Cebu rattan furniture industry

Melquiadesa 'Desa' Canoy is a small woman with the lithe figure and wide-eyed countenance of a teenager. It is hard to believe that her fragile frame can carry a whole bookcase, sometimes together with her one-year old son, from the neighbouring subcontractor's house to her own, and back again after sanding.

Desa is a home-based worker in Mandaue City, the centre of rattan furniture manufacturing on Cebu island. She and her husband were laid off by the rattan factory. As a sander who smooths out the rough rattan surface with hand and sandpaper before painting or varnishing, Desa now earns a maximum of P20 (41 pence) a day for her labours. With these meagre earnings (supplemented by a hundred pesos or so a week from the allowance her husband receives from the trade union where he now works), the Canoys eke out a hard and frugal life, supported by a network of relatives, as is the case for many Filipinos.

Milk for the baby alone costs them P89 (£1.85) a week. Fortunately, they have their own one-room house built on land belonging to Desa's family with their hard-earned savings during better times. They get water from a common artesian well, while electricity is paid for by Desa's mother. They are surviving on their borrowings of about a hundred pesos a month from a small credit cooperative set up by Desa's aunts and other relatives working for a common subcontractor (also an aunt). This relatively better-off aunt, from whom Desa and other home-based workers get the pieces of rattan furniture to sand at a fixed rate, also helps her repay her debts by paying her a fee to mind a small store.

Relatives help in other ways: 'It is good that when our kin arrive from the provinces, they bring vegetables which they distribute among us. This way, we are able to save money which would have gone on buying food.'

Desa is no stranger to hard times. Born to a mother who sold fish in the market, and to a father who for a time engaged in the buying and selling of coconuts and then went unemployed, Desa began her days as a child worker in a rattan manufacturing corporation, straight after leaving elementary school. It was then 1976, and she earned four pesos a day, which she gave to her mother to help buy food for their family of seven. In 1979 she found a better job in another corporation, where she got P24 a day, and was able to attend high school extension classes at night. But after a year, the management said she could no longer continue her studies. Undaunted, she took a qualifying exam set by the Department of Education, as a result of which she became eligible to enrol in college.

Desa did manage to finish one term at the University of Visayas in 1983. By then, she had transferred to still another firm, as the company she used to work for had closed shop due to lack of orders. Desa could not fulfil her ambition to finish her education, because she had to support her two younger siblings through high school. From sander, she was promoted to recorder/receiver. In 1986, when she married a co-worker, their combined income was about P3,000 monthly. With their bonuses, they were able to save enough to build a one-room dwelling, to buy a television set and a cassette recorder, and to afford a baby (plus household help to take care of him at P200 or £4.10 a month). When asked where she gave birth, Desa says she delivered her baby at a private hospital at a cost of P2,000 (£41). She would have preferred to go to the public city hospital, but it was 'overloaded with patients'.

Life had not been too troubled until the second half of 1989, when the company she and her husband were working for put its workers on rotation and finally laid them off in December. The reasons given, says Desa, were standard: 'No more orders, no more raw materials.' In 1989 alone, some 11 factories closed shop, citing more or less the same reasons. This, however, does not mean that rattan furniture production is grinding to a halt. What is happening, according to Desa, is that jobs are being taken out of the factories through community-based subcontractors, for homeworkers to do them at half or even less than half of the prevailing wage rates in the so-called formal sector.

Even the men are doing homework. Desa's neighbours are busy making furniture frames, for which they earn P300-P400 (£6-£8) a month. When asked if women could do the framing and get higher rates compared to the P80-P100 (£1.60-£2.00) a week they receive as sanders, Desa answers, 'Sure, why not? But what will the men do?'

The gender division of labour in rattan furniture making and the resultant wage disparities are so marked that male factory workers have been known to take jobs out for their wives and children to sand for very low pay.

Ups and downs in the rattan industry

Desa is old enough to have observed the ups and downs of the rattan industry in Cebu island. In the early 1970s, concentration was on the export of rattan poles to other countries, because this was an easy way for the traders to earn dollars. With the ban on rattan exports in 1976, the traders began to shift to rattan furniture manufacturing. The industry grew rapidly. Exports rose from an insignificant half a million US dollars in 1969 to $66 million in 1987. Data obtained from the provincial office of the Department of Trade and Industry show 'approximately 125 Cebu-based rattan furniture firms exporting from Cebu with a sub-contractor base of not less than 450 enterprises' in 1987. Then, the conservative estimate for the entire number of workers in the Cebu rattan industry was 40,000. Cebu-based rattan furniture exporters accounted for almost 80 per cent of the value of total exports nationwide.

From the mid-1980s, two trends have become apparent in the industry. One is the increasing unionisation of factory workers, resulting in an appreciable increase in wage rates, even if these still fall far below the official minimum. The second trend, which is in a sense in response to the first, is the rapid rise in the incidence of 'job-out', whereby work is transferred from the factories to home-based workers. The companies' desire to avoid paying higher wages is compounded by the worsening lack of rattan, the most important raw material of the industry.

Rattan is a climbing palm found only in forested areas. It is hard to collect, and its rapid depletion without replanting in the 1970s and early 1980s has forced the Philippines to import rattan from neighbouring countries. But Indonesia stopped exporting rattan in 1987; it is trying to build itself up to replace the Philippines as the major exporter of rattan furniture by inviting Cebu-based manufacturers and workers to transfer there.

The result is closure of many rattan factories. Workers remaining in the formal sector make do with substandard wages and face an increasingly uncertain future.

Facing the future

The days of the rattan industry are numbered, given the crisis in raw materials and the competition posed by Indonesia and other neighbouring countries. The foreign hold on the international market and, to a certain extent, even on local manufacturing (where instances of foreign takeover of ailing firms have been recorded) will probably increase. There has been a shift to more lucrative lines such as stonecraft, which is fast spreading in Cebu. The bargaining power of rattan factory workers will weaken even further, as more and more companies resort to 'job-out' as a survival mechanism.

Desa, who is used to coping with crises, sees hope in a more collective approach to financial problems. While still a factory worker, she was always involved in union work. She is married to a full-time trade unionist who receives a meagre allowance in exchange for his services, but she does not complain or pressure him into getting a regular job with better earning possibilities. She herself has been active in a women's organisation called the KaBaPa (Association of the New Filipina), presently occupied with organising home-based workers with the support of the International Labour Organisation (ILO), and of governmental and non-governmental organisations, including OXFAM. She has done participatory research, translation work, and trainers' training for women, and is looking forward to a time when the home-based workers of Cebu are organised into cooperatives and other forms of self-organisation for their own empowerment. If such associations are in place, home-based workers will be able to shift to other employment as the rattan industry continues to lose its viability.

7

Debt and the agrarian crisis

The Philippines enters the decade of the 1990s with a major agrarian crisis. Agrarian reform, the cornerstone of Marcos' 'New Society' and now the centrepiece of Aquino's democratic restoration, is in disarray. In rice production, the Philippines – once hailed as the success story of Asia – is once again a major importer. The drought that started in the last quarter of 1989 and sizzled throughout the first half of 1990 was aggravated by the sorry state of irrigation infrastructures, thus causing widespread crop losses and consternation among farmers. The rural-based insurgency led by the New People's Army, which began in the early 1970s and was expected to disappear with the change in government in 1986, remains as endemic as before in the more depressed parts of the Philippine country-side, as rural poverty continues to deepen.

These are just some of the manifestations of the agrarian crisis brought about in part by the foreign debt.

Debt and rural development in the 1970s

Rural development was one of the official reasons why the Marcos administration engaged in heavy borrowing, especially during the martial-law years 1972-86. In fact, the Marcos budget ministry declared the 1970s the decade of countryside development, as it borrowed and poured funds into new irrigation projects, supervised rural credit programmes, farm input subsidies, construction of farm-to-market roads, and the expansion of the field-based staff of the Ministry of Agriculture.

The World Bank, Asian Development Bank, and other developmental and commercial lending institutions readily gave financial support to the various rural-based projects of the Marcos regime, whose rural modern-isation programme was compatible with the World Bank's vision of rural development. The major vehicle for this came in the form of the Green Revolution, which doubled, even trebled, output – so long as modern machinery and the right amounts of fertiliser, chemicals, water and other inputs were used. In the absence of the required near-perfect conditions, however, the technology could result in soil exhaustion and other adverse effects on the environment.

To make the Green Revolution work, therefore, the World Bank and other lending institutions supported the national rice programme of the Philippines which called for subsidies for fertiliser, irrigation water, and other inputs; the launching of a massive supervised credit programme with subsidised lending rates; the creation of a National Grains Authority to stabilise grains prices; and the establishment of a range of rural infrastructures, including huge dams and a network of irrigation canals.[1]

Agribusiness expansion

While the government was contracting one foreign loan after the other in the 1970s in the name of rural modernisation, foreign agribusiness corporations were expanding in the countryside. The massive implementation of the Green Revolution opened new markets for transnational firms producing fertiliser, pesticides, herbicides, irrigation pumps, and tractors.

The agricultural modernisation programme was directed mainly at the subsistence and tribal areas, whose main economic activity was food production. In addition, commercial or agribusiness undertakings such as corporate farms, ranches and plantations, especially those producing for export, were encouraged. Not surprisingly, the decade of the 1970s saw a tremendous expansion of plantation agriculture in areas like Mindanao island. There, the production of new export crops like pineapple and rubber spread rapidly; tens of thousands of hectares were converted into plantations or corporate farms, usually at the expense of small farmers and tribal peoples. The same phenomenon occurred in the fishery sector, where the rise of new commercial fishery outfits edged out the small coastal and lakeside fisherfolk.

Deregulation, land reform, and the agrarian crisis

In the early 1980s, the small rice farmers faced a crisis in production, brought about by the rising prices of farm inputs and decreasing support prices for their produce. The sugar and coconut farmers shared their misery, as they were hit by a prolonged crisis in the world market prices for their products, aggravated by the special levies undemocratically introduced for the benefit of a few Marcos allies who monopolised the coconut and sugar industries.

It was against this background that the World Bank pushed for a new development formula for the Philippine countryside: deregulation. Briefly, deregulation calls for phasing out government price controls for farm inputs and outputs; withdrawal of government subsidies for rural

Belinda Coote/Oxfam

Sugar-cane plantation, Negros: Crisanto, aged 10, is the sole wage-earner in his family of six.

credit and for usage of rural infrastructures and farm inputs; removal of government support for monopoly blocs in the sugar, coconut and meat industries; and enhancement of incentives for agribusiness investments.[2] This formula exposes the small farmers to the market on the assumption that they will respond rationally to price signals and optimise their production plans by, for instance, shifting to more profitable crops when the old crops are no longer financially rewarding. To force the debt-addicted and bankrupt Marcos regime to accede to the new deregulation formula, the World Bank offered two structural adjustment loans (SALs) in 1980 and 1982, and a $150 million loan for farm inputs in 1984.

Thus, the government abandoned or drastically reduced its support services for the small farmers. In 1983-85, the Marcos administration had no choice but to accede to every demand of the IMF and World Bank. After the change in government, officials of the Aquino administration simply continued with the deregulation programme, on the assumption that this would be the best for the country.

In 1989-90 the rice crisis burst into the national consciousness as a result of massive imports of rice, a surge in the price of rice, and a fall in rice production. Legislators and farmers' organisations started calling for a review of the deregulation programme. Senator Wigberto Tanada called the decade of the 1980s, which was the decade of deregulation, 'a decade of neglect for the rice farmers'. In his speech before the Senate in early 1990, he warned that without sustained government intervention, the market would be dominated by a Manila-based rice cartel. Heavily indebted rice farmers would not be able to perform well in a market situation, because they lacked not only resources but also technological expertise.

Deregulation also hinders the implementation of the Aquino government's agrarian reform programme. It prevents government from intervening in support of farmer beneficiaries whose lack of capital and market expertise makes them extremely vulnerable to stronger competition. In fact, Marcos' agrarian reform in the late 1970s and first half of the 1980s suffered when the government reduced its support for various programmes, partly as a result of the debt-related budget crisis, and partly in compliance with the World Bank-directed programme of deregulation. The 1980s began to see the phenomenon of 'reverse land reform': the beneficiaries of land reform selling their land rights to old and new rural elites, because of their heavy indebtedness and failure to make farming a viable occupation.

Debt and rural poverty

To sum up, the foreign debt is a major factor in the increase in mass poverty in the countryside. Because of the huge budgetary deficits arising from its gargantuan debt-servicing burden, the government cannot provide for the rehabilitation and expansion of vital infrastructure, the maintenance of price stabilisation programmes needed by small farmers, and the extension of cheaper credit and inputs. This inability to provide timely support to the small farmers is being justified in the name of deregulation.

Industrial and agricultural policies inspired by the IMF and World Bank have also failed to generate the jobs needed by the growing rural population. The rural modernisation programme and the expansion of export-led agriculture have led not only to the growth of big agribusiness but also to the marginalisation and even eviction of small farmers and tribal peoples from their lands.

The small farmers of Nueva Ecija: caught in an ever-tightening squeeze

In the town of Cabiao, Nueva Ecija province, a small group of farmers talk about their daily lives – how much they spend on farming, how much they earn, and why they are almost desperate.[3] Their stories confirm what has been known since the Green Revolution in rice technology was introduced in the early 1970s: the price of farm inputs, mostly of foreign origin, is increasing all the time. The final price of output, in contrast, is not rising fast enough, which leaves rice producers with less and less net income. To continue producing, they have to borrow more and more in order to afford the farm inputs. It sounds very much like a vicious circle.

Ka Berting Manalus, chairman of the Sta. Rita farmers' cooperative, claims that most farmers have to content themselves with harvesting 80 sacks (4,000 kg), one-fifth less than the optimum 100, so they do not have to spend as much on farm inputs. For this modest harvest target, he calculates the total cost of agricultural inputs and services at P10,710 (£223.12), to pay for certified seeds, land preparation, removal of seedlings, planting, removal of weeds, weedkillers, pesticides, fertiliser, harvesting, hauling, land rent, irrigation, thresher, and a contribution to the cooperative's development fund.

Ka Berting says a farmer must invest P4,700 (about £98) for preliminary or pre-harvest expenses in order to remain in rice production. But where does someone like him, who lives a hand-to-mouth existence, get such an amount? Certainly not from the banks, which, for a P3,000 (£62.50) loan at

Negros: the poor, excluded from the good land by sugar-cane plantations, have to grow their food crops on the most marginal land — by the roadside, in this case.

12-18 per cent interest, insist on so much red tape (like certifications from the Department of Agrarian Reform, the Department of Agriculture and other government agencies) that it is not worth the time and effort. According to Ka Berting, out of the 270 farmers in Sta. Rita village, only 35 get loans from banks.

The moneylenders, therefore, are having a heyday. Some charge 20 per cent a month, or 250 per cent a year, but want to be paid on a daily basis. Most farmers cannot afford this, since they do not earn anything till harvest. They prefer the more costly 'takipan' form of credit, in which the loan and interest are repaid after the four-month cropping season. The interest typically works out at 25-40 per cent a month.

Assuming that there is no drought or infestation, how much can the farmers expect to net from their harvest? Ka Berting says that most farmers harvest around 80 sacks (4,000 kg), worth P16,000 (£330). If the P10,710 (£223) spent on inputs and services, as well as the P5,000 (£104) paid in interest on a P5,000 (£104) takipan loan are subtracted, net income per hectare is only P290 (£6). Assuming that the size of the farm totals the average three hectares, a farming family earns P870 (£18) per cropping season, certainly a paltry sum, given the current cost of living.

The net result is that many farmers are already giving up their land. 'Most of the farmers during the time of Marcos are no longer the farmers now,' says Ka Berting. 'Right now, the government wants us to produce the needs of the nation, while we cannot even meet our own needs. This means most of us cannot pay our loans, can no longer get loans, and are consequently forced to sell our right to cultivate the land.' So the effects of the national debt problem are felt in a credit squeeze at the grassroots level.

Ka Ambo Santos adds, 'Our families have to eat and live during the planting season. And there's an average of seven people in each family! There's a saying round here: "We've already eaten the harvest – and it's not even harvest time yet". Yet, as Cory Aquino says, "We have to keep our word of honour".' (There is a hint of sarcasm in Ka Ambo's voice here.) 'We have to pay our debts. We have to pay direct taxes, and indirect taxes too, when we buy the goods of other producers. We are then forced to sell our land to people who convert it to a fishpond or some other business, while we become workers in the cities.'

The drought takes its toll
These indeed are the worst of times. Aside from financial woes, farmers are experiencing the effects of a protracted drought, made worse by environmental degradation and government neglect. The dams are getting drier as a result of massive deforestation and siltation, while the massively inefficient irrigation systems supply water to only one-quarter of the total irrigable areas in the country. There is a link here with the national debt: the scramble for foreign exchange encourages the export of forestry resources, and the resulting denudation of the land destroys watersheds. Furthermore, the huge debt-service burden prevents the government from improving and expanding irrigation services.

'This April we could only gather one-third of what we used to harvest,' Ka Cora Manalus, one of three women in the small farmers' group, interjects. This means an income of only P3,600 (£75). Ka Cora, unmarried and now in her 40s, practically manages the family farm since her brother, a full-time community worker who gets P300 a month as village councillor, is too busy to do it. The land, however, is in the name of her brother, as the male head of household. Ka Cora also takes care of their ailing 80-year-old mother, whose recent kidney operation and medical expenses for the next half-year or so are projected at P2,000 (£40).

So how does Ka Cora stretch the income from such a lean harvest? She scrimps on food, coffee, sugar, soap and shampoo. She saves on electricity (she no longer watches television) and yet she complains that her bill for ten kilowatt hours still amounts to P20 or 40 pence (compared to P7.50 per 15 kilowatt hours in the early 1980s, before the debt crisis exploded and triggered sharp increases in public utility rates). She gets extra income from the chickens, pigs and vegetables that she raises, income she reserves to pay for the farm inputs for the next planting season.

The discussion then shifts to problems in the community, which the farmers also connect to the burden of the foreign debt. Ka Ambo, for example, observes that while a doctor, nurse and dentist visit them once a week, they no longer receive free medicines, as they used to during the Marcos era. 'One of the reasons for this, as I understand, is that as much as 44 per cent of the national budget automatically goes to debt payment. Consequently,' he explains, 'we usually don't go to see the doctor. Instead, we go to the *herbolario* (herb doctor) or to the faith healer; they prescribe medicinal plants which we can easily find around here.'

Ka Miling Dizon shifts the discussion to the water problem. 'Most farmers believe that the drought during the dry season and the floods during the rainy season are the work of God,' he observes. 'I explain to them that our irrigation system is not well-planned and organised. The dikes of the fish ponds hinder the flow of water during the rainy season. There is not enough water during the dry season, because the government can't afford to maintain and improve irrigation facilities.'

Ka Ambo interjects: 'We have drought and flood because the government allows loggers to cut trees and shave the mountains clean.'

Hope in a cooperative

In the face of such grave problems, how do the farmers respond? They have just formed a cooperative, in order to get access to credit and other facilities, especially from government agencies, which prefer to deal with just a few people. As a result of their initial efforts, they were able to acquire a thresher andsmall rice mill through the National Food Authority. Through the cooperative, too, says Ka Berting, 'We hope to find a lawyer to help us in our land case.' He explains that under the land reform programme of the Marcos regime, they paid their landlord P5,697.50 (£120) per hectare, but under the Comprehensive Agricultural Reform Law (CARL)[4] of the Aquino administration, their former landlord has reopened the compensation issue in accordance with CARL's principle of 'fair market value'. The price per hectare they had paid the landlord as a result of Marcos' land reform is now deemed insufficient and even insignificant, compared to the P65,000 (£1,300) per hectare that the same landlord is charging them under CARL.

The future holds many trials, but Ka Berting believes that if small farmers unite through their cooperatives, they stand a better chance of survival.

The reponse of farmers' organisations to the debt crisis

How do farmers' and rural workers' organisations see the foreign debt problem? How do they connect their other concerns – agrarian reform, environmental degradation, the need for a comprehensive national rice policy – to the foreign debt? What do they want done, and what forms of action have they taken to move forward? In a roundtable discussion with leaders of member-organisations of the largest farmers' network called the Peasants' Forum, some of the answers crystallise.[5]

— *The debt is connected with the rising cost of farm inputs, because of creeping devaluation and therefore rising inflation and higher costs of imports.* (Devaluation is one of the standard prescriptions of creditor institutions, principally the IMF.)

Ka Trining Domingo, vice-president of the women's organisation KaBaPa, says rice seeds now cost P18 (37 pence) per kilo compared to P8.00 (16 pence) last year. The price of each bag of fertiliser rose by about P50 (£1); it was the same with every bottle of pesticide. The cost of renting a tractor also went up, because spare parts for machines have also gone up. The cost of diesel oil for farm use has increased by 70 per cent in twelve months.

Ka Paeng Mariano of the peasants' movement Kilusang Magbubukid ng Pilipinas (KMP) relates these escalating prices to the floating exchange rate and floating interest rate.

— *The debt is responsible for the rising cost of living and lower living standards, especially for agricultural workers; and it means more work for rural women.*

Ka Loring Ayupan, chairperson of the peasant women's federation Amihan, explains that the problems of rural communities can be traced to the conditions contained in the Letter of Intent. As a result, she says, 'We have to bear the higher cost of electricity and water; we also have to pay more taxes. Prices of goods and services are skyrocketing. Women have to budget, even if there is nothing to budget; women have to work more, at home and in the fields, to make both ends meet.'

Ka Trining adds that women have to do more unpaid work on the farms, so that the family can save on labour expenses. They prepare the meals and drinks of the farm hands and take them to the fields. They keep watch when the harvest is being hauled from farm to road. They also do the weeding. Most of the agricultural workers who do the planting and harvesting are women, Ka Trining continues. Each one earns between P30 and P35 (62-70 pence) a day for planting in Nueva Ecija, and this does not go very far. The planting season lasts only for about 20 days in one area, giving maximum earnings of P600 (£12), and there is no work afterwards. During harvest time, the harvester gets one-ninth of the harvest (one sack out of every nine). She can earn the equivalent of one sack (P250 or £5) in three days, but the longest she can work is about 15 days. The most she can earn therefore during the whole harvest season is about P1,250 (£26).

Agricultural workers belong to landless or marginalised farming families. Ka Trining observes, 'Many are reduced to eating rice and vegetables, with salt or bagoong [fermented shrimp].' The really desperate give up their land, abandon farm work, and seek work somewhere else – as domestic helpers, for example.

— *Policies imposed by foreign creditors have adversely affected Filipino farmers, while benefiting foreign interests.* 'Almost all the government subsidies for farmers have disappeared,' says Ka Vic Fabe of the peasant group PAKISAMA. 'The entry of foreign products into the Philippine market became easy,' he adds. 'For example, in Metro Manila, imported apples are everywhere. If you put the imported apple beside the local mango, the mango is more expensive. The local Filipino product is left unbought and allowed to decay, which is one reason behind our current economic difficulties.' Imported fruit dumped on the local market can be sold more cheaply.

Ka Paeng maintains that the priorities of the government favour the needs of foreign interests, rather than the needs of the people. For example, he explains, 'It gives priority to the production of export crops for foreign markets, while neglecting local agriculture, health, education, and other social services that can respond to the needs of our people.'

Ka Rudy Sambajon of the fisherfolk's federation PAMALAKAYA claims that 'Development programmes for farming and fishing communities, infrastructure for electricity and potable water, as well as social services cannot reach the countryside, because the great bulk of the people's money is used to pay for the debt.'

— *The debt worsens environmental problems like the protracted drought.*

'The connection is quite simple,' Ka Rudy explains. 'Aquino merely continued the Marcos policies on foreign borrowing, as a result of which our natural resources became open to foreign exploitation. Foreigners used Filipino loggers to cut down our forests and export the logs.'

The result of forest denudation, according to Ka Rudy, is that rivers silt up and watersheds are destroyed. Little water can be stored in the dams, aggravating the effects of the long drought which Agriculture Secretary Senen Bacani says damaged crops worth P315 million (£6 million) and caused opportunity losses of up to P1.75 billion (£36 million).[6]

The food blockade: farmers fight back

Ka Louie Paterno, general secretary of the farmers' coalition SANDUGUAN, says the food blockade they spearheaded in the third quarter of 1989 was the most dramatic action so far launched by farmers to prove that they have the will to defend their livelihood, even if it means placing the country's food security in jeopardy. Their concerted action highlighted the problems of rice farmers, which were worsening as a result of the price of unmilled rice (stagnant since 1984) and the price of farm inputs and other commodities (rising rapidly because of inflation). The situation, Ka Louie adds, was aggravated by foreign-imposed policies such as privatisation and deregulation, even more underscored by the contents of the Letter of Intent issued in March 1989. Farmers were neglected and sacrificed, while foreign and local businessmen, especially the traders, benefited.

'We saw that whatever we did, the government merely ignored us; so

L. Freeby/Oxfam

Rice farmers in a paddy field near Mercedes.

we thought of launching the food blockade,' explains Ka Louie. 'Then we realised that the country's food security was really very shaky, because if we persisted with our blockade for at least a week, there would have been panic in Metro Manila. That much, the military, too, had to acknowledge.'

The demands of the food blockade, says Ka Kikoy Baltazar of the federation of agricultural workers AMA, were summarised in the protest symbol: a hand with five fingers, the fingers standing for a support price of P5.00 (10 pence) per kilo of unhusked rice; a P5,000 (£104) loan for every hectare to be cultivated; a P5 billion (£104 million) fund for the National Food Authority to enable it to buy rice from farmers at the official price; P5 billion (£104 million) for rural development; and the abolition of the five-cavan (250-kilo) irrigation fee.

The blockade lasted for several days. According to Ka Trining, many women joined the mass action in Sta. Rita, Bulacan, and actually positioned themselves in the front lines. 'The military hesitate to use violence if they see women in front of the barricades,' she explains. 'Agriculture Secretary Sonny Dominguez was forced to go there himself because the blockade, which positioned itself on the superhighway north of Metro Manila, really prevented middlemen's trucks loaded with rice from passing through and reaching the metropolitan area,' she continues.

Even in the follow-up mass actions in front of the Department of Agriculture, women formed part of the picket lines. The growing militancy and unity of farmers' groups forced no less than President Aquino to meet with them and grant their demand for a P5.00 minimum price for unmilled rice.

In the process of lobbying, rallying and picketing for a comprehensive national rice policy, farmers' organisations of various political persuasions grew closer together. Three major groups which did not cooperate before have begun talking to each other and making common positions. These are the SANDUGUAN, the Federation of Free Farmers (FFF) and the Congress for a People's Agrarian Reform (CPAR).

Ka Tino Bancug of the farmers' coalition LAKAS firmly believes that the peasants, if they organise themselves, can exercise considerable influence on government policy. They could exert pressure on the government not to pay the debt, in the same way that they obliged it not only to sit up and listen, but also to grant some of the farmers' demands.

8

Debt and the fishing communities

Filipino fisherfolk, numbering eight million, live virtually on the edge of existence, as the water systems which comprise the sphere of their livelihood become increasingly monopolised, polluted, and destroyed. The national debt is a major factor in their tragedy, because it is the linchpin of the development model which sacrifices their interests in favour of big foreign and local concerns; and the debt encourages practices that harm the environment. The connections may seem distant, but they are real. They are also full of bitter irony.

The Philippines, an archipelago of 7,100 islands, used to be considered one of the richest fishing grounds in the world. The country contains 211.6 million hectares of water bodies – coastal, oceanic, as well as inland. It used to rank twelfth in fish production globally, and under good conditions more than two million metric tons of fish and other sea foods could be caught annually from Philippine waters.[1]

Still, Filipino fisherfolk are hungry and poor. One explanation is that they have less and less access to what used to be communal fishing grounds. Fish pens fence them out and are hindering their passage to 'free' waters. Commercial fishing operators, with their huge nets and advanced fishing gear, beat them to whatever is unfenced, and corner almost all of the catch. In the island of Palawan, for example, a small fisherman can expect to catch only one-seventieth of the haul of a commercial operator.

Many of these sophisticated fishing concerns are foreign, specifically Japanese. Fisherfolk always cite the RP-Japan Treaty of Amity, Commerce and Navigation signed in 1973 as an onerous one, because it allowed Japanese merchant and fishing vessels to enter Philippine waters and catch all the fish they want, while Filipino fisherfolk take the leftovers. Another Marcos edict that fisherfolk still resent is Presidential Decree 704, which encourages the export of fisheries products by private businesses, and identifies fishing as a preferred area of investment for foreigners.

Another explanation for the poverty of the fishing communities is that Philippine waters can no longer yield good catches for the small fisherfolk because of rapid environmental degradation. Here, debt figures in two ways. First, the export of forestry, mineral and fishery resources to earn much-needed dollars has resulted in extensive siltation, pollution, salination and destruction. Second, the intensifying poverty associated with debt-fuelled development has driven marginalised fisherfolk towards using cyanide, dynamite, and other harmful methods of fishing. Deep-sea divers, including children, are obliged to seek employment in muro-ami fishing, a hazardous occupation which involves pounding coral reefs with rocks in order to drive fish into waiting nets.

Of the estimated half a million hectares of mangrove forests which line Philippine coasts, only 146,139 are left, as a result of fishponds and other forms of aquaculture encroachments. Mangrove forests are important because they serve as breeding, feeding and nursery grounds for fish and other aquatic life.[2] In 1988, the total aquaculture area was estimated to have increased to 224,264 hectares, which means more and more mangrove forests are being converted to fish farms. For every hectare thus converted, a maximum of 1.4 metric tons of fish and shrimp is lost annually in terms of potential production. Worse, fish farms occupy the former fishing grounds of small fisherfolk, who are forced to fish somewhere else in ever-diminishing space. They cannot be employed in the fish farms, which are capital-intensive, not labour-intensive. These fish farms cater to the foreign market by engaging in prawn culture, in accordance with the government's export-oriented fishery policy, encouraged by Japanese loans.[3] Lately, inland prawn farms have been criticised because they cause the destruction of surrounding fields through salination.

Only 25 per cent of Philippine coral reefs are in good condition, and some 50 per cent of them are in 'advanced stages of destruction'.[4] These reefs serve as homes and breeding grounds for fish. They are being destroyed by siltation due to soil erosion caused by forest denudation, by the use of cyanide and explosives to get quick returns in fishing, by pollution from assorted sources, and by quarrying for construction, aquarium and export purposes.

The decline in coral reef production by at least 37 per cent in the last 30 years has resulted in the loss of seafood that could feed three million Filipinos. Ironically, fishermen destroy coral reefs and small fish in the course of dynamite fishing (about 50 per cent of fisherfolk reportedly resort to this), so they can catch more and thereby live through the next day. While they are doing this to meet their immediate survival needs, they are destroying the very source of their sustenance over the long term. Thus, the cycle begins: poverty breeds destruction breeds more poverty.[5]

Many of the country's lakes and rivers are dying because of siltation resulting from overcut forests, and pollution coming from industrial plants, from mine tailings, from fertilisers and insecticides used in agriculture, and from domestic wastes due to inadequate garbage disposal and sewage systems. Laguna de Bay, Southeast Asia's largest inland lake, formerly a source of livelihood for some 11,000 fishing households in 27 lakeshore towns, is now dying and can support fewer and fewer fisherfolk.[6] About 40 of the country's 400 rivers are 'virtually dead'.[7]

A third explanation for the fisherfolk's continuing and intensifying poverty is that government programmes neglect, marginalise, or displace them. There is no fishery reform, as there is no real agrarian reform. Social services barely trickle down to fisherfolk, who are among the poorest of the poor. Infrastructure development for big foreign and local business displaces fisherfolk. Examples of this are the building of a 100-kilometre road dike around Laguna de Bay, and the plans for converting the CALABAR (Cavite-Laguna-Batangas-Rizal) region into an industrial area with funds from the Japanese International Cooperation Agency (JICA) through the Philippine Aid Plan.[8]

The ten-year CALABAR industrialisation plan, costing $735 million, includes the building of roads, ports, railways, telecommunication and transport facilities, power-generating plants, export-processing zones and mass housing. Foreign investors are expected to benefit most from it, and the government is expected to support it because of the expected dollar income from exports that would help to pay the foreign debt. Within this grand design, Laguna Lake will serve as a source of water, irrigation, and power. Will fisherfolk be provided for? Only in terms of possible employment, which is unlikely, because in the first three years available jobs will be at inaccessible supervisory, technical, and advisory levels.

According to Ka Rudy Sambajon of the fisherfolk's federation PAMALAKAYA, only three per cent of the lake will be left to fish in. He says, 'Even if we join all our boats together, they won't fit in just three per cent of the lake.' Yet it is in the interests not only of the fisherfolk but also of the entire Filipino people to maintain the lake as a fishery resource. Fish is their major source of protein, and Laguna Lake's maximum potential yield can very well provide 20 per cent of total national production. More fish would be available in the local market, the price of fish would go down, more people would be able to afford it, and the 400,000 people who directly and indirectly depend on fishing in Laguna Lake could sustain their livelihood.[9]

John Clark/Oxfam

Bataan Province: the future of small-scale fishing is threatened by commercial operators who convert the mangrove forests (important fish-breeding grounds) into fish farms.

Unfortunately, government priorities and programmes seem to be at odds with the interests of the small fisherfolk. These policies merely perpetuate conditions under the Marcos regime, when projects supposed to develop Philippine fisheries and help fisherfolk proved to be problematic, ineffective, and even counter-productive. One major example was the Biyayang Dagat programme, meant to provide credit for aquaculture development and for new boats and gear for small fisherfolk. 'Out of the targeted 700,000 beneficiaries, only 6,892 fishermen were able to avail themselves of loans amounting to P83.5 million within the period 1979-1982' – when a total of P792 million should have been available as of the early 1980s.[10] The reasons for this low performance included stringent loan requirements, and the fisherfolk's inability to provide collateral and cope with high interest rates.

The new five-year Fisheries Development Programme for 1990-1994, on which the Aquino administration has embarked with a $140 million loan mainly funded by Japan through the Asian Development Bank, has more adverse implications. Shorn of rhetoric, 'Its general thrust is to rehabilitate our marine resources to increase fish production for export, particularly to Japan, while depleting local market supply,' according to a critique of the Programme.[11] Its sector programmes aim to develop and expand commercial fishing and aquaculture through 'exploration of tuna fishing in the West Pacific; construction of infrastructures and other fishing facilities; census of all existing fishponds; and revision of license and lease fees ...'. It seeks to privatise government-owned cold-storage, warehousing and market facilities at fishing ports, which 'could be in line with the government's promise to the IMF ...'.[12] It will rely on expensive foreign consultants, and oblige the government to provide counterpart funding, another drain on the national budget.

What's in it for small fisherfolk? The Programme makes some mention of assistance towards developing diverse sources of income, which may have the effect of displacing fishing communities, making it easier for big commercial fishing operators to monopolise the fishing industry in collaboration with foreign interests.[13]

Fisherfolk organisations want a lot more than this. They demand nothing less than a Comprehensive Fishery Reform Code based on the following principles: 'Filipinization of the fishing industry; democratization of use and management of fishery and aquatic resources; national fishing industrialization; promotion of the ecological balance of the natural resources; provision and delivery of social services; and advancement of a genuine agrarian reform.'[14]

Lupo Masaclao: from fisherman to shoemaker

Mang Lupo Masaclao refuses to believe that Laguna Lake is dying. He remembers, not too long ago, when the lake was generous to all, giving steady sustenance to countless communities living on its edges. 'You didn't need a college degree to live on the lake,' says Mang Lupo. 'If you were industrious and you had the will to sustain your family, all you had to do was get into the lake and harness its bounty.'

In the mid-1970s, it was still possible for fisherfolk like Mang Lupo to derive a relatively comfortable income from the lake. Their minimum daily earnings totalled a hundred pesos (compared to the minimum wage of only eleven pesos in 1978) and could provide more than the basic needs of their families. 'We even had savings,' Mang Lupo recalls.

The situation drastically changed when fishpens were constructed all over Lake Laguna, leaving the small fisherfolk very little room to pursue their livelihood. They started to organise against the fishpens, their numbers in the town of Binan alone reaching about 600. In Malaban village, where Mang Lupo lives, they carried out a long and bitter campaign marked by persistent dialogues with government agencies in charge of the lake, and marred by violence and witch-hunts directed against leaders.

The fisherfolk's struggle, which reached its peak in the early 1980s, was crowned by apparent victory in 1983. The fishpens were dismantled before their eyes. The military came, no longer to hound them but to make sure the fishpen owners did not make good their threat to liquidate those responsible for the dismantling. 'You should have seen the fisherfolk then,' Mang Lupo recounts with a broad smile. 'They were crying and laughing at the same time.'

But their joy was short-lived. The next problem they had to face, according to Mang Lupo, was the closure of the Napindan Channel which had connected Laguna Lake to other water bodies. As a result, water in the lake became murky and could no longer sustain as much life as it used to. The lake was dying, they were told, and, as they were fisherfolk, it seemed like a death knell for them, too.His experience in 1984-85 convinced Mang Lupo that fishing in the lake was no longer a viable livelihood. 'Whenever we went out to fish, our catch was just enough to pay for the diesel fuelling our boats,' he explains. Soon he found himself shifting to catching shrimp instead of fish, because this did not require going far into the lake.

Problems with Laguna Lake

The unfortunate turn of events did not lead to apathy and despondency. The fisherfolk continued their campaign for their right to the Lake as a source of life and livelihood. Their efforts focused on the reopening of Napindan Channel, culminating in a *lakbay-lawa*, a march around the lake dramatising their sentiments.

The closure of the Napindan Channel is just one of many issues highlighting environmental degradation and the continuing conflict among various interests competing to exploit the lake. The Napindan Hydraulic Control Structure was actually built in 1983 to help make the Lake a source of potable water for Metro Manila by the twenty-first century. The structure was supposed to prevent toxic materials from the Marikina river and salt water from Manila Bay from flowing into the Lake. The effect, however, has been disastrous for fisherfolk. Mangrove trees along the lake shores disappeared; water-lilies proliferated; fish shelters, fish food, and fish growth drastically decreased. The older fisherfolk even attribute outbreaks of fish disease to the Napindan closure.[15]

Pollution and siltation have compounded the fisherfolk's problems. As Mang Lupo explains, 'Even if Napindan is able to control the flow of toxic wastes from some sources, what about those originating from Laguna province itself? What about the factories dumping industrial wastes? What about the pesticides and chemical fertilisers used in the fields? What about the municipalities and subdivisions throwing garbage and sewage into the lake?'

If current trends are not reversed, the lake is threatened with death by the year 2000, as a result of industrial pollution and rapid siltation caused by forest denudation and soil erosion. Among those still hopeful that the lake can be saved are Mang Lupo and his group, one among many fisherfolk's organisations in the lakeshore towns.

Looking for alternatives

However, Mang Lupo and his fishermen's association called SIGASIG (a Filipino word connoting industry and determination) are realistic enough to venture into shoemaking as an alternative to fishing while the Lake's status continues to deteriorate, dragging the fisherfolk's living standards downwards.

Mang Lupo looks back to better times in 1983, when the fishpens had just been dismantled, and when the peso had not yet been drastically devalued due to IMF pressure. Then, a daily fishing income of P80 could still provide rice and fish for the family; vegetables could be raised and harvested from the garden.

Today, he says, for fisherfolk or shoemakers to survive, they have to borrow money for food. They get short-term loans from usurers, traders, and retail store owners who are still sympathetic to their plight. In the case of shoemakers, 'They get advances from their employers, not knowing nor caring if their wages for the coming week are sufficient to cover these.' Thus, the cycle of perpetual indebtedness begins.

In the early 1980s, Mang Lupo relates, fishing families could look forward to a meal of high-quality fried fish, and sometimes even to soup with some meat in it. Today, even the lowly *galunggong*, the cheapest medium-sized fresh fish in the market, is a welcome sight. 'I was able to send most of my children to school through the Lake,' Mang Lupo reminisces. 'I always tell them that life can only improve if they finish some education and get good jobs afterwards. Not like me – I can only be a fisherman; I finished only first-year high school, while my wife reached only third grade.'

Mang Lupo has six surviving children out of the original ten. Two died soon after birth, and two died from sickness in childhood. He is proud of two children who finished high school in a private institution (thanks to the Lake), but he is sad that they still cannot get good jobs because they do not have influential backers. One more child is struggling through third-year high school by earning through vending, one stopped in the third grade, while the two remaining ones have an uncertain lot at the elementary level.

Mang Lupo notices a decrease not only in educational opportunities for the poor, but also in the services available in the public health clinic. He recalls that under the past administration, doctors came frequently and medicines were available, if not freely given. Today, he says, it is all on prescription, without considering the sick person's ability to buy the prescribed drugs.

Foreign domination

Mang Lupo also has very strong feelings about the general deterioration in the living standards of the people, especially of fisherfolk, because of the power and privilege given to foreign corporations and creditors. 'The price of almost everything is going up,' he laments. 'Even matchsticks are now being produced and marketed by foreigners. Foreign products are killing products we can produce ourselves. Look at what happened to our native fruits. All the talk of progress and development being bandied about is empty; in fact that "development" is a great tragedy for poor people like ourselves.'[16]

'In fisheries,' he continues, 'foreign control and influence is quite strong. Those who benefit most from our fish ports and deep-sea resources are not

Filipinos, but big foreign fishing concerns who edge us out of the most lucrative areas. Even what we use for fishing is imported and tends to get more expensive when the dollar gains against the peso through devaluation. The net from Taiwan that we used to buy for P50 (£1) now costs almost P200 (£4). And of course, we have to reckon with the rising cost of diesel for our fishing boats.'

Mang Lupo is also suspicious of the foreign-supported infrastructure that is being proposed. The road dikes that are being built around the Laguna Lake through the Japan International Cooperation Agency (JICA) are considered a threat by fisherfolk. 'Where will we dock our fishing boats?' Mang Lupo asks. 'What we need,' he says, 'is to build our own industries so we do not have to spend our dollars. Instead of dollars flowing out, we can even make them flow in.'

The birth of an alternative
Consistent with their belief that Filipinos can make it under their own steam if given the chance, Mang Lupo and his group called SIGASIG formed a cooperative to engage in shoemaking. This alternative livelihood became virtually the main option in his community, starting in 1983, when the fish catch suddenly declined. By the late 1980s, about 90 per cent of the working population in Malaban village were already engaged in shoemaking, either as owner-manufacturers or as workers in cottage-based or home-based manufacturing. From a fledgling industry producing slippers and wooden shoes as a side occupation for fisherfolk, shoemaking became the main source of livelihood in Malaban – but under conditions which exposed the people to exploitation by monopolists and middlemen.

To provide an alternative production and marketing arrangement where the producers can purchase raw materials in bulk and market their products to realise higher profits to share among themselves, the SIGASIG Fishermen's Association formed a shoemakers' cooperative. They had a series of consultations with OXFAM, which had previously supported community organising efforts in the area. OXFAM asked the Cooperatives Foundation of the Philippines, Inc (CFPI) to do a feasibility study on the shoemaking project and, after positive advice, decided to fund the project, with CFPI providing training support. Fixed assets and working capital to the tune of P317,971 (£6,624) were made available to the cooperative, of which amount about P100,000 (£2,083) was considered a loan.

The cooperative has 27 male and 12 female members. They built the workshop, of simple bamboo structure, themselves, and installed the major tools and equipment (sewing machines, hammers, cutters, moulders, a dryer, grinder and cleaning machine). Labour is divided by gender, in the sense that the men do the soles and related jobs in the workshop, which fetch about P45-P55 (£0.93-£1.04) a day, while the women do the upper parts with their sewing machines at home for P20-P25 (41-52 pence) a day. The combined incomes of men and women are expected to benefit the whole family.

The role of women in SIGASIG is still quite limited. They remain very much within their culturally prescribed gender roles. As wives of fishermen, they seldom do actual fishing, and are mostly confined to marketing and household work. As shoemakers, they do their sewing at home. They are quite reticent; Mang Lupo describes his wife as too shy to be interviewed. This may soon change, however, with the formation of a women's organisation among them. OXFAM, together with another local partner (SHIELD), is supporting this organising effort. At the same time, OXFAM is trying to enlist the support of the men in SIGASIG for the women's cause by raising their awareness on gender issues.

Since SIGASIG was formed as early as 1978 to serve the fisherfolk's cause, and since it has a track record of service and influence in the community, it had no problem in securing outside support. Mang Lupo himself had been a community leader. He was instrumental in having public toilets built along the lakeshore. An artesian well and free medical services for the community through networking are among his other accomplishments.

People still come to him for help whenever they are aggrieved. One important human rights case was brought to him by relatives of eight fishermen allegedly massacred by the drunken guards of a rich fishpen owner in July 1989. Among them were Aling Mary Almazan, whose four sons were killed in the massacre and who is now reduced to gathering clams and selling them for P20 (41 pence) a day to help sustain her large family.

Since the SIGASIG cooperative is very new, it is still too early to tell whether it will work. Even now, its members are facing problems posed by intermittent power cuts and escalating costs of imported raw materials, controlled by the Chinese. Income from shoemaking is also expected to be seasonal, peaking at Christmas and at the start of the school year. Mang Lupo is still thinking of multiplying livelihood possibilities, with shoemaking only one among many. He still looks to the lake with hope.

9

Debt and the tribal Filipinos

A development model fuelled by debt and favouring the powerful can only wreak havoc on the lives of people who by history and tradition have always remained outside the mainstream of national life. This is exactly what is happening to some 4.5 million tribal Filipinos belonging to over 40 ethno-linguistic groups, found in the remote mountains and hinterlands of the country. They were neither conquered by the Spaniards, nor (in the south of the country) converted to Islam, and they have somehow maintained their indigenous cultures in the face of colonial exploitation and the corrosive influence of lowland penetration.

There are six major tribal Filipino groups: the more than two million Lumads who include all the non-Muslim tribes of the southern island of Mindanao; the one-million strong Cordillera peoples living in the Northern Luzon mountain range; the Caraballo tribes, numbering around 160,000 and inhabiting the Eastern Central Luzon mountain range; the nomadic and dark-skinned Agta and Aeta, also about 160,000, who were among the country's earliest inhabitants; the Mangyans of the island of Mindoro, about 111,000 in all; and the Palawan hill-tribes, totalling around 120,000.[1]

These tribes derive their sustenance and livelihood from upland farming, from sometimes sophisticated rice culture, from hunting, fishing and gathering, from small-scale mining, and from handicraft. Their ancestral domain includes resource-rich areas which have been attractive to loggers, miners, and plain carpetbaggers. The entry of foreign corporations, private business concerns, construction companies and other non-indigenous interests into tribal territory has marginalised the tribal peoples, driven them out of their land, and destroyed their homes and habitat. Growing number of landless rural poor are encroaching farther and farther on upland forests, which has the same devastating impact on the tribal communities. Lowland invasion and land-grabbing, often akin to a slow and creeping ethnocide, has been aggravated by the hunger for foreign exchange which demands the unlimited export of logs and minerals in order to service the national debt.

Dams before people

The pattern of encroachment became pronounced in the 1970s, at the height of the Marcos regime, when aside from the upsurge of commercial mining, logging and farming activities by non-indigenous concerns, huge hydro-electric dam projects funded by foreign creditors were proposed to complement and support private 'development' efforts. The affected tribes did not take this affront lying down. In 1975, the Bontocs and the Kalingas, in a letter to then World Bank President Robert S. McNamara, communicated their objection to any World Bank assistance to the Chico River Basin Development Project. 'The reason,' according to them, 'is simple. The project would wipe us out as a people! At least ten Kalinga settlements and six Bontoc settlements will be devastated as a result of this dam project.'[2]

The tribal people's opposition to the Chico Dam was a courageous and bloody one. Even while the area was still being surveyed, Kalinga women walked into a surveyors' camp and dismantled their tents. They were arrested and detained, together with their men, who were also resisting the project. But they pushed on and eventually prevailed: the Marcos government and the World Bank eventually cancelled the project.

The other tribes have not been so fortunate. The T'Boli people of Lake Sebu in the province of South Cotobato also wrote to the Asian Development Bank to register their opposition to any form of ADB support for the Lake Sebu Dam project. According to them, 'The proposed dam will flood our most precious land and destroy our food and source of livelihood which we have worked so hard to produce.' The land, they say, is precious: 'Our ancestors were born and were buried here ... We would rather be drowned here and be buried with our ancestors than live far from our homeland.'[3] But Lake Sebu appears on the 1990 list of 51 existing and proposed hydro-electric dams which are expected to affect 2.58 million tribal Filipinos.[4]

Dams are not the only bane. The government plans to build a geothermal plant on Mount Apo, the sacred mountain of the Lumads. About 480,000 of them will be affected by a project which completely ignores their right to their ancestral domain. Mount Apo, the highest mountain in the Philippines, is also noted for the diversity of its flora and fauna; it has been declared a national park, a sanctuary for the fast-disappearing Philippine eagle, and a recognised 'environmentally significant area' by the United Nations and ASEAN. The geothermal plant, therefore, threatens not only the Lumads, who have marched in

Peter McCulloch/Oxfam

A T'boli tribeswoman weaving in her village near Lake Sebu.

protest against it, but also the wealth of species which claim the mountain as their home.[5]

To sum up, power-generation projects assume that the welfare of indigenous Filipinos must be sacrificed in the interests of 'development'. These projects are meant to provide the energy requirements of industries in which the tribes participate little, or not at all.

Focus on the Cordillera region

In the Cordilleras, the exclusion and displacement of the indigenous peoples is better documented. Large-scale logging in the provinces of Kalinga-Apayao, Benguet and Mountain Province threatens the last remaining forests in the area. Logging concessions in the 'pine belt' have deprived many communities of access to forest resources, so people have to resort to over-exploitation of remaining communal forests, 'illegal cutting of pine trees in concession areas or falling back on the remnants of the mossy forest' only found in the highest and remotest areas. Concession holders make no effort to reforest the area, which leads to even faster depletion of forest resources.[6]

Already, the effects are alarming. According to one source, about half of the Cordillera region's forests are denuded, and soil erosion from slight to severe affects more than a third. Because of over-logging, the flooding which came in the wake of Typhoons Goring and Openg in 1989 led to death and unprecedented destruction of property and crops in the valleys.[7]

Large-scale mining is concentrated in the Cordillera province of Benguet, which is responsible for some 73 per cent of Philippine gold production, 46 per cent of silver output, and 22 per cent of copper production. Transnational corporations and their Filipino partners control the mines, whose profits go out of the Cordilleras, if not out of the country. The mine owners prefer to employ lowlanders, and suspect indigenous peoples of 'highgrading' or stealing ore. The Ibaloi and Kankana-ey tribes are often confined to small-scale or pocket mining, a livelihood which their ancestors had engaged in even before the colonisers came.

Large-scale mining has many adverse effects, including deformation of the natural landscape, soil erosion, reduction of water supply (with the dropping of the water table), siltation, chemical pollution of rivers, and destruction of plant and aquatic life. There is no measure yet of the extent of the damage. One environmentalist notes that mercury, lead, cadmium, arsenic and cyanide flow into water bodies used for irrigation and domestic purposes.[8] The adverse impact on the health and agricultural produce of the indigenous communities still has to be measured.

Although it may be too extreme to lay all these ills at the door of the foreign debt, there is a connection which, no matter how indirect, cannot be denied. The country's dire need for dollars to pay its foreign creditors impels it to continue exporting its irreplaceable resources, including mineral products, even if mining firms engage in environmentally disastrous activities. In the 1970s, the Philippines exported $4.168 billion worth of mineral products, and in the 1980s, $4.783 billion worth of the same.[9]

Debt and ethnic poverty

Other connections to the debt become visible when we look at the poverty of the Cordillera peoples and the paucity of basic public utilities and social services in the region. The wealth and the taxes squeezed out of the region do not return to those who live there: the resources which flow into the central government coffers are spent somewhere else, principally on debt payments.

As late as the 1980s, about four-fifths of Cordillera households did not have electricity. Almost two-thirds of pre-school children were malnourished. Many school buildings were dilapidated, not a few beyond repair.[10] About two-thirds of the population surveyed in two Cordillera provinces considered themselves poor, despite the 'very simple life' already considered adequate by indigenous peoples. One study describes their 'simple meals, which normally consist of plenty of rice or sweet potato and boiled or sautéd vegetables', a large proportion of which they grow themselves, and their 'very simple clothes'.[11] One can only speculate what could have been done to augment this 'simplicity' if the country were not saddled with a huge debt problem and could afford to attend to the needs even of its marginalised peoples.

Indigenous peoples against open-pit mining

On the long and winding road from Baguio City to the Antamok area, one is struck by the contrast between the lush pine trees which line the periphery of the Baguio tourist centres and the depressingly brown mountainscapes of Antamok seen from a distance. The mountains have been scraped bare by open-pit mining, and the price is paid by the indigenous peoples whose livelihood depends on the mountains.

Leaders and members of the Luneta and Loakan Pocket Miners' Associations, together with key initiators of the Timpuyog Dagiti Umili Iti Itogon (Organisation of Itogon Residents) firmly oppose Benguet Corporation's P600-million open-pit mining operations, known as the Grand Antamok Project (GAP). In the words of the community's leaders: 'We used to be sound asleep. Now we are wide awake. We now realise that our mountains will disappear if we do not make a move against open-pit mining. So we formed ourselves into human barricades.'

Open-pit mining threatens to scrape the mountains flat, scoop up the earth in millions of metric tons and dump them into surrounding areas, divert a major river and channel it elsewhere so that the company can mine its bed, dry up water sources, and destroy the land on which the indigenous Ibaloi and Kankana-ey peoples built their small-scale mines and grow their food.

As a young pocket miner put it during a dialogue with officials of the Environmental Management Bureau of the Department of Environment and Natural Resources (DENR), 'If we don't have any land to mine, we will starve and will thus be forced to steal. The big mines can't employ us all; we are not machine operators, which is what the mines need.'[12]

In the words of a statement issued by Timpuyog: 'Antamok, which has been a mining area of the indigenous peoples for hundreds of years, will be buried.' With it, the relationship of the Ibaloi and Kankana-ey to land traditionally theirs will also be buried. As they say, 'We have been extracting gold from the mountains and rivers long before the foreign conquerors came.' They have derived food and sustenance from tilling the surrounding land. And now they will be disinherited almost completely, with their ancestral domain subjected to wholesale destruction which will mean the deformation of the natural landscape, more denudation, erosion, siltation, and pollution from hazardous chemicals used in open-pit mining, which flow into the rivers that provide irrigation water and a habitat for fish and other forms of aquatic life.

'We are being asked to leave our mines, but where shall we go?' asks one leader of the pocket miners. 'This is our livelihood. The company may have the legal papers for this land, but it came from our forefathers. We tell them you can have the papers, we can have our land. But we accept their legal claims. They should not pressure us too much.'[13]

Benguet Corporation has been in the area since 1903, starting out as a purely North American concern. By 1941, it was the biggest mining company in the country ('the second largest under the American flag') and its main stockholder 'Judge' John Hausermann was called 'the American Gold King of Asia'. In the 1970s, sixty per cent of Benguet shares as well as its overall management underwent a form of Filipinisation. Filipino names – Ongpin, Ayala, Romualdez – began to be associated with it. Government subsidies poured into it.[14]

After almost nine decades of extracting gold in the richest mining area in the Philippines (the Cordillera region, to which Benguet belongs, accounts for 75 per cent of all the gold extracted in the country), Benguet Corporation now finds it difficult to make so much money from its underground mines. The cost of digging deep into the earth has become prohibitive, prompting the corporation to attempt open-pit mining, where excavations are made on the earth's surface to expose the veins of gold ore.

The Timpuyog statement laments: 'The corporation squeezes every ounce of gold and even goes to the extent of destroying the forests and the natural contours of the earth in its feverish search for gold so that the few top officials in the corporate ladder can live like kings. It pays taxes to the central government, leaving our communities underdeveloped.'

By contrast, in the words of the indigenous pocket miners, 'We take only what we need for survival, and share our blessings with others through our *canaos* [feasts].'

A way of life under threat

Until the open-pit mining issue exploded, the Ibaloi and the Kankana-ey peoples left Benguet Corporation pretty much alone. Certainly they were conscious of discrimination, because the company preferred to hire lowlanders as 'corporate miners' and tended to accuse highlanders of stealing gold from the mines. But they were content to coexist with the corporation while they had access to their small-scale family mines (shallow tunnels called adits), from which they could earn an estimated P2,000 (£41.60) a month per family with the gold they could sell at P220 (£4.50) per gramme. Young and old, men and women, are involved in these mines. During the summer, children on vacation from school work in the tunnels or volunteer to cook, in exchange for a few pieces of gold ore. They can get as much as one thousand pesos (£20.80) each per season, enough to buy clothes and other needs. One fifth-grader already expresses concern about open-pit mining. 'If that happens, where will I work in order to earn money to buy a new pair of pants and shoes?' he asks.[15]

Women increasingly work in the small-scale mines, as they become displaced from their traditional farming tasks by the lack of water for their once-verdant rice paddies. They attribute this to disturbance of the water table as a result of underground tunnelling by the big mines. Women miners are mostly seen crushing the gold ore before milling. They sit on their haunches in a circle, pounding the ore with what look like large hammers. More and more of them are also joining the men doing strenuous work in the low-oxygen tunnels, to eke out the family income.[16]

But now, with open-pit mining, family-based pocket mining is threatened, and if plans succeed, about 20,000 pocket miners and gold panners will lose their livelihood. For this reason women and children have been present at the barricades set up to prevent the trucks of Benguet Corporation from ferrying their load to and from the GAP area.

The campaign to protect the Cordillera environment began much earlier, with the community and education work done by the Cordillera

Committee for Environmental Concerns (CCEC), founded in March 1988. The CCEC, which is supported by OXFAM and other non-governmental organisations, highlights the extent of environmental degradation in the region and tries to prevent it. The CECC has focused its efforts on open-pit mining, and has been instrumental in mobilising people and public opinion against GAP.

A public issue
During the first mass action staged in September 1989 by hundreds of small-scale miners ordered to leave the Camote Vein area by the Benguet Corporation to make way for GAP, the CECC was there to witness the company's bulldozers and payloaders scrape the mountainsides.[17]

Since then, the issue has become a public one. In October 1989, the Itogon Sangguniang Bayan (municipal board) passed a resolution urging the Department of Environment and Natural Resources (DENR) 'to cancel all permits granted to and revoke all applications for surface mining' within the area, because this will 'aggravate the deplorable conditions of rivers, the wanton destruction and exploitation of natural resources, and the elimination of rich agricultural lands'.[18]

In November 1989, flying rocks from a dynamite blast near the Keystone vein of Benguet Corporation's open pit damaged 12 houses and wounded a nursing mother, provoking near violence from angry residents.[19] The DENR ordered the company to compensate the victims, who had not been properly warned of the blasting activity.[20]

In February 1990, Itogon municipal officials once again expressed their opposition to surface mining. Benguet provincial officials also revealed their apprehension in a resolution stating that 'permission (for) open-pit mining should only be granted as a last resort and after sufficient protective and safety measures are installed to avert and forestall any damage to the people and the environment'.[21]

The local officials' sentiments were, however, contradicted by Benguet Representative Samuel Dangwa, who said members of Congress and other national officials were not inclined to favour GAP's closure, because of the dollars it could generate. According to reports, Dangwa made remarks to the effect that 'BC's mining activities help bring in the much-needed foreign exchange that can help pay off the country's almost US$30 billion debt'.[22] Benguet Corporation itself is reportedly heavily indebted to Bankers Trust, Bank of America, and the Export Development Corporation.[23]

Towards the end of February 1990, the protest of the small-scale miners began to peak. Together with residents of the six affected villages of Itogon, they flocked to the public hearing on the open-pit mining issue, conducted by the DENR. The number of people who attended was estimated at 2,500, most of them expressing opposition.

The barricades and beyond
On 28 February 1990, human barricades began to form on key roads to the open-pit mine-sites, armed with a stop order from the DENR. As related by their leaders, miners and residents of the affected villages, including women and children, turned up with posters, streamers and placards, and turned back BC trucks carrying gold ore. 'We were prepared for a long fight, and devised a schedule of shifts whereby each person would have to be at the barricades one day and one night a week. People brought their own food or went home for their meals.'[24]

The company complained that it was losing about a million pesos a day because of the barricades. Soon, the military came to serve the temporary restraining order issued by the Regional Trial Court in response to BC's request. Twenty-seven leaders were named in the order, but they and their followers remained undaunted. The barricades remained.[25]

In the face of increasing pressure, the protesters have moved to strengthen their internal unity and external support. The Timpuyog (Organisation of Itogon Residents) took shape, bringing together community leaders from the six affected villages, who with the CECC sit on the Steering Committee. The Advocates' Coalition Against Open-Pit Mining went down to Manila to picket the office of Benguet Corporation. Journalists have visited the barricades to write sympathetic stories for the local and metropolitan press.

It is now a test of wills. On one side is a powerful but highly indebted corporation with strong local and foreign connections, whose destructive operations are rationalised by the dollar earnings they bring in. On the other side lie the indigenous peoples of Itogon, who are finally awake to the 'development' which threatens their survival.

10

Debt and the urban poor

Nobody knows how many squatters there are in the cities of the Philippines, but everyone knows their numbers are multiplying. An official source, the Presidential Commission on the Urban Poor, claims that there were four million at the end of 1988, 1.7 million of this number in Metro Manila alone.[1] Another official source, the National Housing Authority (NHA), claims that 406,000 households are 'squatters' or slum dwellers. If this figure is multiplied by six (which is the average family size), the estimated total squatter population adds up to 2.43 million, more than a third of Metro Manila's seven million inhabitants.[2] They congregate in some 415 or more squatter colonies, reported the NHA in 1985. But there are more, according to organisations representing the urban poor in 1987, who counted about 600.

Who are they? What are their problems, needs and aspirations? According to one author:

> The urban poor inhabit the small pockets of unoccupied land at the periphery of subdivisions, along railroad tracks, estuaries, dumpsites, sidewalks, marshlands, cemeteries, marketplaces, bridges ... and other dangerous sites. They have unstable sources of income, irregular employment and are lacking in the most basic facilities such as health, education and other social services. They live in extremely congested and unhealthy neighborhoods with inadequate water and sanitation facilities. Being poor, their children have very limited educational opportunities. Malnutrition and diseases are prevalent and commonly a cause of high rates of child mortality.[3]

The urban poor are defined as people whose monthly income falls below the urban poverty threshold of P3,005 (£62.60) for an average family of six (1989). They provide basic services as domestic helpers, laundrywomen, street sweepers, garbage collectors, mechanics, plumbers, carpenters, etc. Many of them are self-employed vendors, hawkers, and scavengers, home-based and sweatshop workers who invigorate the 'informal' or 'underground' economy said to be responsible for as much as 43 per cent of the Gross Domestic Product. The more fortunate who work in the 'formal' sector engage in low-paid, low-skilled jobs in factories, in ports, and in the transportation and construction industries.

Many of the urban poor are squatters. A squatter, according to Philippine law, is 'Any person who, with the use of force, intimidation or threat, or taking advantage of the absence or tolerance of the landowner, succeeds in occupying or possessing the property of the latter against his will for residential, commercial or any other purpose'. Thus, any squatter is under constant threat of being evicted or prosecuted; any squatter's home is always in danger of being demolished. The anguished faces of slum dwellers whose homes have just been knocked down by demolition squads are a common sight on newspaper pages and television screens.

Many of the urban poor are homeless. They form part of the 60 per cent of urban households who do not own the land on which their houses stand. Nationwide, 3.5 million families and 21 million individuals are homeless.[4] They are paying the price for the country's shortfall of housing units, estimated at 1.66 million nationally. As we shall see later, this shortfall has something to do with the severe financial constraints which prevent the government from pursuing an adequate housing programme. And such constraints are related to the tremendous drain in resources caused by debt service.

Less housing for more people

In Metro Manila, there is less and less housing for more and more people. The annual need for new housing in the metropolis is estimated at 200,000 units, while for the whole country the figure reaches 400,000. Yet, for the period 1975-1988, the National Housing Authority (NHA) reported constructing only 12,891 new housing units for low and middle-income families (7,544 in Metro Manila and 5,347 elsewhere). This is a mere drop in the ocean of need.[5] The six-year National Shelter Programme of the Aquino government set a target of 106,993 new housing units to be constructed, with funding support of P4.2 billion. In 1988, only 2,396 units were constructed.[6]

Makeshift dwellings called *barong-barong* mushroom in many parts of the metropolis. Overcrowding is a fact of life for half of Metro Manila's inhabitants who live in dwelling units with a floor area of less than 30 square metres each, a cramped space often shared with other families.

And there is no way of stemming the tide of people pouring into the metropolis, whose population swelled from an estimated one million after World War II to the seven (some say ten) million today. Most of the new inhabitants come from the rural areas, where the encroachments of agribusiness and the increasing concentration of land in the hands of a few have the effect of marginalising the peasantry and increasing the army of landless rural poor. The lack of employment and income opportunities in the countryside, in some areas aggravated by armed conflict, pushes many rural dwellers to try their luck in the cities. Here, they take on any job, no matter how lowly or ill-paid, or engage in marginal income-generating activities like scavenging or vending. Almost all of their earnings are spent on food, with almost nothing left for shelter. So they live in makeshift dwellings in squatter colonies bereft of water, electricity and sanitation, and deprived of health, education and security services.

Partly because of the huge financial drain exacted by debt service, the government lacks the resources to implement a serious urban land reform and housing programme for 'underprivileged and homeless citizens', as mandated by the 1987 Constitution. Government, for example, was able to provide only P428 million (£8.91 million) in equity and subsidy to the 1988 financial resources of the NHA, totalling P1.236 billion (£25.75 million). The rest had to be generated from project beneficiaries, from the sale of lots, and from foreign borrowings (P125.318 million or £2.61 million).[7]

The demands of the urban poor
The role of foreign creditors, principally the World Bank, in the government's housing programme has been prominent since the Marcos period. And the record has not been very positive. The first project of the World Bank was the on-site upgrading of the Tondo foreshore area in Manila, which has the highest concentration of slum dwellers in the country. This benefited only a few, particularly the middle-income earners who could afford to pay for the cost of improvements. Also, during the process of census-taking, many of the original dwellers were somehow dropped from the list of beneficiaries.[8]

Representatives of the urban poor themselves, in a consultation held in May 1986 at the Ateneo Centre for Social Policy and Public Affairs, criticised foreign-aided housing projects in no uncertain terms:

> On the level of negotiating with global institutions (such as the International Monetary Fund and World Bank), our government plans and agrees to launch projects and loans with oppressive

policies. Ordinarily, inappropriate and exorbitant costs are borne by the country, especially by the poor, due to such agreements. Various payments (development costs, interest costs, etc.) rise without beneficial effect due to the policies imposed by the lenders. Added to this is the hiring of foreign consultants who get exorbitant dollar salaries, and yet do not fully comprehend the concrete needs of the Filipino poor. Also to be noted is the dictation of standards in housing construction and design under the project which costs a lot of money and is therefore beyond the reach of the poor.[9]

In response to this problem, they proposed that the 'government desist from receiving loans from international funding agencies such as the IMF-WB which support projects that are inappropriate and too expensive for poor people'. As regards loans already incurred, the contents of the agreement should be laid open, so that the people affected would be fully aware of the responsibilities they would be placing on themselves.

The urban poor have other demands. Proposals of the National Congress of Urban Poor Organisations include a 'moratorium on demolitions and all payments on existing housing projects and land transfers'. They ask the government to expropriate lands they are currently occupying, so that these may be communally owned by them. They call for in-city relocation of urban poor families if relocation is inevitable. As regards social services, their priority is clearly health, as they demand not only free health services and facilities, but also free training and education in primary health care. They want core housing units and projects to be developed and paid for by urban poor beneficiaries according to their means. Such housing schemes, they say, should be supported by local funding agencies 'and not be dependent and controlled by foreign agencies such as the IMF and World Bank'. Last but not least, the urban poor demand adherence to the democratic principle of 'participation by those concerned in the community in the decision-making processes'.[10]

The women of Tondo learn to read, write, and survive

Narrow lanes framed by rusty walls lead to a compound of makeshift houses – home to about a dozen families. The focal point of the compound is a running tap, around which women are sitting on their haunches and washing clothes in basins spread out on the ground. Beside them, a young girl covered with soap suds takes a bath fully clothed, while some other children just play or linger around their mothers. The surrounding homes are wooden shanties on stilts, averaging four square metres in size, and each sharing common walls.

Most of the women of the compound apparently make a living from their laundry work. They earn about P300 (£6.25) a month, the poorest of the urban poor who do the washing for others just slightly better off than them. Aling Bella has four children and a sick husband, who was forced to give up his job; she relies on her son who works at the pier to help tide the family over. Aling Patring's husband is blind. He goes out to beg to help support their two children.

The two other women – Aling Adriana, who sells sleeping mats on the sidewalk when the police are not looking, and Aling Fely, who sells chicks and toys in front of the school when no guard is in sight – also have families which they maintain and help support on irregular incomes. Aling Adriana, who calls herself a 'widow' (her husband is still alive, but no longer lives with her), is lucky if she makes a hundred pesos a day. Sometimes, she says, she sells nothing, especially during the rainy season when sidewalk vending becomes too difficult. Aling Fely says P60 (£1.25) a day is a good take for her, when she is lucky enough not to be victimised by the school guard's extortion activities.

All four women have one thing in common – they are students in MAKAMASA's women's literacy project situated in Magsaysay Village, Tondo, Manila, which started in October 1987 and continues to make an impact on their lives, with assistance from OXFAM and the Australia-based International Women's Development Agency (IWDA).[11]

These women are no longer young; they had to endure cutting comments from their families and neighbours when they started to learn to read and write at such a late age. Aling Bella's children used to tease her with statements like, 'Mother, you are acting like a Grade One student!' When they realised she was serious about her studies, they stopped making light of her efforts.

One-third totally unemployed

MAKAMASA is now thinking of branching out from literacy to income-generation. The main problem in Magsaysay Village is unemployment, which translates itself into very low family incomes. The women estimate the number of totally unemployed at about one-third of the working population. The men who have work are pier hands or street vendors, selling anything from T-shirts to cosmetics, and earning from P50 to P70 (£1.45) a day. Because of their low level of schooling, they cannot compete for scarce factory jobs, which generally require high-school education.

Some of the women are street hawkers, forever on the lookout for the police, who often extort money from them. The really desperate do laundry work. Others make do by raising pigs. Aling Teret, a MAKAMASA member, says she has to wake up very early, travel all the way to Divisoria market and gather the decaying left-over vegetables to feed her pig. 'I'm a garbage woman every morning,' she says, with a wink.

But no, they protest, nobody in their community ever goes into prostitution. 'If ever, they go abroad as dancers or entertainers, so nobody really knows what they are doing.' One youngish, childless MAKAMASA member at this point confesses to having applied for work as a domestic abroad. Everyone in the group is against it: 'You will only be victimised by fake recruiters; you will only be raped,' they argue to dissuade her.

The burden of carrying the family through a daily financial crisis falls mainly on the women. They make sure that the daily rice staple is still on the table, then scrounge around for the vegetables and cheap fish to go with it. (For the very poor, fish sauce, soy sauce, fermented shrimp, or salt suffice to go with the rice.) They learn herbal medicine so that if anyone falls ill, they do not have to go to the doctor or buy expensive drugs. They raise chickens and pigs to eat or sell. They are forever on the lookout for anything which can earn or save money.

The MAKAMASA women dream of having cooperative income-generating projects, but they have neither the capital nor the market. One going concern – the making of big bags made of cloth with a sewing machine donated by IWDA – is so far restricted by the lack of orders. During the Christmas season of 1989, Ka Sela reveals, they embarked on producing home decor called 'Sarilaya bird' for relatively well-off buyers. But the response was lukewarm; they ended up selling the birds to sympathisers at P20 (41 pence) each, with a mark-up of only P3. Despite the setback, they are proud of their creative output, and still keep samples in their office to show to visitors.

Whatever projects are envisioned – garments, soap, and Christmas crafts are some of the products they are exploring – must be well thought out, with a ready market in mind. The women need training in cooperativism, marketing, and record-keeping. At the same time, they have to deal with problems threatening their families and their community.

Impending eviction

Aling Bella fears impending eviction from her home of 20 years. The owner of the compound where she and the four other students of the literacy project live is threatening to have their shanties demolished.

Aling Florita, vice-president of MAKAMASA, describes the continuing problem of defective drainage in Magsaysay Village: blackish, foul-smelling fluids ooze from unexpected places (especially during the rainy season when the floods come), because the roads were not planned well enough to allow for passage of water which used to just flow through the area. She also suspects some corruption among the personnel of the National Housing Authority (NHA) who took charge of building the drainage system.

Aling Florita also airs the grievance of many village dwellers whose rent on the land on which their homes are built has been arbitrarily raised by the National Housing Authority. Residents now refuse to pay the jacked-up rates. Meanwhile, their overdue accounts, plus interest and fines, pile up at the NHA. How is the NHA expected to react? 'Well, they can padlock our homes, but they haven't done that yet,' they say.

Another problem concerns illegal electricity connections, as a result of which some residents with legal connections are overbilled for power consumption that is not solely theirs.

What about the social services?
As the discussion turns to social services, the women become more agitated. Aling Bella, whose only daughter goes to a public high school in Quezon City, complains about the prices of uniforms which can only be bought from the school: 'One skirt costs a hundred pesos!' She earns P300 (£6.25) a month from laundry work. But perhaps the school needs the cash from the sale of uniforms for things that can no longer be supplied by the debt-ridden government? Maybe, says Aling Bella.

Aling Florita, for her part, relates an incident which made her very angry. She was trying to get her child's clearance from a public high school. Her child, she explains, is sickly, and she thought it best to send him to the countryside, where she hopes he will regain his health. The teacher in charge would not give her the necessary papers without a bribe. She brought the case to the principal, who confronted the teacher and ruled that the mother should be given the necessary papers without further ado.

Aling Florita's tale of woe sparks an animated discussion about problems with public service workers like teachers, who keep marching down the streets, forgetting about the service they should be giving to the people. Teachers have had to become hustlers, they observe, selling things to their students – anything from food to clothes.

'Perhaps because the government doesn't give them the salaries they need to live decently,' someone interjects. 'Perhaps,' the women say, but

Rosalinda Pineda-Ofreneo

Feli Capelar and her daughter at home in Magsaysay village, Tondo, Manila. Feli is a leader of the MAKAMASA women's organisation.

sceptically. It seems that they cannot imagine how someone who earns more than P3,000 (£62.5) a month (the minimum wage for teachers) can still be dissatisfied.

When the topic switches to medical service, Aling Bella observes that the existence of a health clinic with a permanent doctor does not really mean much if one cannot afford the medicines the doctor prescribes. 'Drugs are no longer given out for free,' she complains.

'What about the DSWD [the Department of Social Welfare and Development], which is supposed to serve the poorest?' someone asks. The women claim it is now too difficult to get any help from the DSWD. They mull over the observation that the DSWD can no longer afford to operate, because of its low budget. The women are groping towards an understanding of foreign debt, and the way they are paying for it through taxes directly and indirectly paid. They volunteer their own examples. 'We pay taxes every time we use cooking gas. Every time we board a bus, because our fare covers the cost of gasoline.' And so on. And so on.

Issues of global economics no longer seem so distant.

11

Towards an alternative strategy for debt and development

The debt problem is too important to leave to the government to decide. Its impact on the people is too severe for them to ignore; in fact, their participation is the prerequisite for any real solution. In the Philippines, people are responding to the debt problem in many different ways.

The Freedom From Debt Coalition

The establishment of the Freedom From Debt Coalition (FDC) is perhaps the most significant initiative in developing a broad-based people's response to the worsening problems stemming from the Philippines' debilitating external indebtedness.

According to Filomeno Santa Ana, FDC secretary general, steps towards its formation began as early as the first quarter of 1987, when the Aquino government was still at the height of its popularity, and the euphoria arising from the 1986 'people power revolution' was still palpable. The new administration was then beginning to deal with the foreign debt problem and negotiate with foreign creditors.[1]

'The immediate demand of the group who would later convene the FDC,' Santa Ana recalls, 'was transparency: the release of the specifics of the foreign debt transactions, as well as information on how much debt was owed by Marcos' allies and under what terms their loans were made. The group focused on the popularisation of the debt issue and stressed the role of people's organisations.'

They were in a sense continuing the initiatives of the 1970s and the early 1980s, when prominent academics, opposition politicians, and action-oriented groups critical of the Marcos regime campaigned against its dependence on foreign loans, with the consequent loss of national independence, amid signs of massive corruption tainting these loans.

The founding congress of the Freedom From Debt Coalition was held in March 1988. Since then, the FDC has attracted into its fold 144 organisations from a broad range of political viewpoints, including church groups, academic and professional bodies, and community organisations, which have come together in order to work jointly for the realisation of a people-created debt policy. The points of unity are contained in FDC's 'minimum programme':

1   The government should declare a moratorium on foreign debt service payments until acceptable terms, which do not sacrifice the country's economic development, are won in new rescheduling agreements.

2   It should disengage from loans that do not benefit the people, particularly those tainted with fraud, and reject any liability for private borrowings.

3   Foreign debt service should be limited to not more than 10 per cent of export earnings, to enable the country to finance economic recovery.[2]

In a strategic plan worked out in its latest congress held in July 1990, FDC describes its vision of 'a free and democratic Philippines where debt is not a burden but rather an instrument of growth and equity within the framework of a progressive national economy, where the resources and fruits of production are equitably distributed within the context of a just international economic order'. Its mission, according to the plan, has two aims: to 'work towards the realisation of a people-oriented debt policy through the building of a Filipino freedom from debt constituency, strengthening international linkages and partnerships, and linking the debt policy to a comprehensive alternative development strategy'; and to 'work with other national broad formations, coalitions and organisations to realise genuine and sustainable development in the country'.[3]

Since its founding, the FDC has engaged in popular education and mass campaigns, policy research and analysis, lobbying, and networking nationally and internationally. It has combined the expertise of prominent academics, sympathetic legislators, highly-skilled researchers and economists, and dedicated social development workers deployed in many institutions and non-governmental organisations, with the mass reach and practical experience of trade unions, peasant movements, and other people's organisations.

FDC has staged mass actions to dramatise its positions on debt and debt-related issues. In July 1989, it launched a colourful parade complete with floats, music bands, and circus characters to coincide with the opening of Congress, during which the President delivered the traditional state-of-the-nation address. The parade highlighted the FDC's alternative interpretation of the state of the nation, touching on foreign debt and the economy, agrarian reform, human rights, military bases and nuclear weapons, and alleged graft and corruption.

In November 1989, the FDC organised a march to the Lower House to press for the approval of the Lagman Bill, calling for a debt-service cap of 15 per cent of export earnings. This widely supported bill already had the signatures of more than three-quarters of the members of Congress, but pressure from the executive branch was preventing its final passage.

Another FDC demonstration, held in August 1990, was a march to Mendiola bridge in front of Malacanang, the seat of the presidency. Mounted shortly after the disastrous July earthquake, the march dramatised the call for a debt service moratorium as an appropriate humanitarian response to the country's plight. In its latest mass action, staged in February 1991, FDC protested against the newest Letter of Intent by marching towards the Central Bank, the usual site of 'secret negotiations' between Philippine finance officials and IMF representatives.

Among the FDC's more significant popular education efforts was the Campaign Against The Letter Of Intent (CALOI), launched shortly after the LoI had been issued in the first quarter of 1989. CALOI emphasised six points of opposition:

- Only a small group of officials participated in negotiating, formulating and adopting the LoI.
- The LoI will result in a rise in the price of rice.
- It will lead to new taxes.
- It is inconsistent with the government's avowed goal of poverty alleviation and employment generation.
- It commits the people to continue making massive debt service payments.
- It glosses over the structural reasons for the country's dependence on foreign funds.[4]

Aside from CALOI, FDC's other popular education activities include seminar-workshops on such topics as privatisation and economic policies for the poor. FDC has published primers on the Philippine debt crisis and on women and debt, as well as newsletters and small brochures which form part of its public information series. It has co-sponsored sectoral gatherings like a congress on women and debt, and a luncheon forum with businesspeople.

In August and September 1990, FDC held press conferences to publicise the results of the research on fraudulent loans, conducted by six of its member institutions. This is part of the larger strategy of disaggregating fraudulent loans from legitimate ones, and mounting national and international campaigns against paying tainted loans. Concentration at this point is on loans for the Bataan nuclear power plant, a white elephant located in territory prone to earthquakes and volcanic eruptions. Originally priced at $500 million, the cost of the plant escalated to $1.1 billion and then to $2.3 billion. The country pays $350,000 a day in interest payments alone, apart from P200 million a year for maintaining a useless monster.[5] Aside from exposing the massive corruption surrounding the Bataan nuclear plant in the Philippines, the FDC has made an international issue out of it.

The FDC's influence and expertise are recognised both nationally and internationally. FDC leaders are always invited to public hearings and to national and international conferences, including UN-sponsored ones on human rights and on women and debt. In fact, the United Nations Special NGO Committee on Development has given its endorsement to the FDC Programme, and the managing director of the International Monetary Fund, Michel Camdessus, has met with Professor Leonor M. Briones, president of FDC.

FDC's international network is already extensive. It is a member of FONDAD (Forum on Debt and Development), together with several Latin American research institutions. It receives support from Bread for the World (Germany), and CEBEMO and NOVIB (the Netherlands); OXFAM (UK and Ireland) and Christian Aid help to fund its research and educational publishing programme.[6] And it is working closely with groups in Switzerland in its campaigns against fraudulent loans.

Legislative initiatives

Much of the lobbying on debt has focused on the bicameral legislature, which is empowered under the 1987 Constitution to propose and approve all budgetary appropriations. Only the Philippine Congress can appropriate funds for debt service. In practice, however, the executive branch, through the Central Bank and the Department of Finance, has been monopolising the formulation of debt policy and the strategy for negotiating with foreign creditors. The results are very unpopular.[7]

To counteract this, Congress, despite a presidential veto, passed an Act in April 1989 creating a Joint Legislative-Executive Debt Council. According to proponent Senator Alberto Romulo, he had to rise on the floor and deliver a speech so that the Senate would override the veto, and, fortunately, all his colleagues supported him.[8] The Act gives the legislature a means of influencing debt policy, and emphasises sustained growth, equity, stabilisation, national sovereignty, and public participation as guiding principles for the work of the Debt Council.[9]

The Council, however, can only recommend, given its research and advisory capacity. Furthermore, most of its members come from the executive branch. The end result is that the final decisions are still made by the President and her negotiators.[10]

Even then, it still seemed worthwhile to improve the composition of the Debt Council by adding representatives from non-governmental organisations as 'part of a genuine commitment to people's participation in the formulation of public policy'. This is the gist of Senate Bill 1178, which the Freedom From Debt Coalition strongly supported.[11]

The most important legislative initiatives so far are those proposing a cap on debt service. Senate Bill 535, sponsored by Senators Romulo, Gonzales, and Maceda and approved 'overwhelmingly' in November 1988, proposed the limitation of debt payments to 20 per cent of export earnings for the years 1989-1992. Its counterpart bill in the lower chamber, House Bill 25835, is spearheaded by Congressman Edcel Lagman and signed by 158 members of Congress, more than three-quarters of the House. The bill aims to limit appropriation for external debt service to l5 per cent of the country's export earnings. Furthermore, it aims to repeal presidential decrees issued under the Marcos dictatorship which provide for automatic appropriation for debt service and executive discretion on the matter. These decrees, although superseded by the 1987 Constitution, are still in force and comprise the main excuse for preventing Congress from exercising its power to make all appropriations, including that for debt service.

The Lagman Bill, however, has not been formally approved by the House. Congressman Ramon Mitra, Speaker of the House and leading light of the majority party identified with the President, indirectly expressed opposition to the bill through a caustic remark tantamount to saying that the members of Congress who co-sponsored the bill would sign anything – even toilet paper.

Tension between the legislature and the executive branch continues on the debt issue. Despite the President's refusal to heed their call, Senators Romulo and Saguisag have been campaigning for the sense of Senate Resolution 161, which urges the government to 'suspend, avoid, and disengage' from further payments for the balance of the fraudulent loan spent on the $2.3 billion Bataan nuclear plant. In the aftermath of the earthquake of July 1990, both chambers approved a joint resolution calling for a thirty-month debt service moratorium to enable the country to rebuild destroyed areas and recover from severe economic losses. President Aquino and her negotiators refused to listen, apparently for fear of adverse reactions from foreign creditors over such a unilateral action.

Similar tension between the executive and the legislature was more recently apparent in the aftermath of the volcanic eruption of Mount Pinatubo. The Finance Secretary, Jesus P. Estanislao, has estimated that the cost of relief, rehabilitation, and reconstruction in areas affected by the volcano will exceed the cost of repairing the damage done by the 1990 earthquake (estimated at P15 billion, or £305 million). (The damage and the opportunity costs caused by the volcano are still mounting, as Mount Pinatubo continues to rumble indefinitely.) This latest calamity spurred the legislature, in the new national budget, to propose a debt cap of 20 per cent of export receipts. In response, President Aquino exercised her right of veto.

Towards an alternative development strategy

Proponents of all the short-term approaches to the debt crisis are united in proclaiming the need to link the debt policy to a comprehensive alternative strategy for development. Some general principles which might underlie this alternative development strategy have already been identified, to which divergent and emergent social forces may contribute their ideas in the process of building a broad consensus.

One source articulates three principles: *the national interest*, which means the Filipino people must harness their vast natural and human resources for their present needs and maintain them for future use, for which they must protect their right to set economic priorities; *poverty alleviation*, which means stressing 'the majority's right to life fit for human dignity', and working for 'the reform or transformation of unjust economic and social structures that pamper the rich minority and burden the poor majority'; and *democracy*, which means real participation of the people in the political process.[12]

All these principles, it is argued, are violated by external debt and adjustment policies and programmes which are made and implemented 'without the knowledge, participation and consent of the affected', especially when these entail much hardship and sacrifice on the part of the people who are made to suffer for crises they are not responsible for.

On the level of national rights, campaigners claim that these policies and programmes violate the right of countries to development, to national sovereignty, and 'to work out their own paths to development, taking into account national interest'. According to Professor Leonor Briones, FDC President, 'In the case of indebted countries, national sovereignty is compromised, since it is the lending institutions which determine economic policies and shape development models as conditionalities for lending. In extreme circumstances, it is these lending institutions who practically manage the economic and financial affairs of these countries.'[13] Basic therefore to any long-term alternative strategy is the assertion of 'the right to development as a human right', the recovery of national sovereignty, and the institutionalisation of democratic processes.

The main task for the campaigners is to raise public awareness, and to consolidate and mobilise a decisive constituency for an alternative development framework based on the creation of a balanced, well-integrated, industrialised and sustainable domestic economy geared first and foremost to meeting the needs of the people, and only secondarily to catering to the demands of the global market.

With such an economy, campaigners claim that the Philippines can solve its basic problem of 'excessive reliance on imports',[14] particularly industrial machinery, equipment and raw materials, and lately even food and other consumer needs. Establishing firm foundations for Filipino industries would mean producing these imports internally and therefore minimising the need to go into debt just to get the dollars to pay for these imports.

Agrarian reform
Campaigners argue that basic to industrialisation is the implementation of genuine agrarian reform, to give the peasantry and agricultural workers access to and control of land, towards increasing food production for the populace as well as raw-material production for local industries. This would also lead to the creation of a strong domestic market to absorb and support local products.

The demand for an agrarian reform has reverberated throughout decades of peasant unrest in the Philippines. The most broad-based initiative, however, was launched in May 1987 with the formation of the Congress for a People's Agrarian Reform (CPAR), a coalition of 12 national organisations of peasants, fisherfolk and rural women. CPAR set down the following aims of a people's agrarian reform programme:

1   To transfer landed wealth and power over the land and its produce to the actual tillers.

2   To free and develop the productive powers of agrarian workers, farmers and fishermen from the forces that deprive them of resources and initiative.

3   To develop the mechanisms for people's empowerment by creating autonomous decision-making bodies in the rural communities.

4   To promote nationalist industrialisation by widening the national market, rechannelling the agricultural surplus into industrial investments and labour for industrial development, and establishing self-sufficient local industries controlled by the rural workers.

5   To conserve the natural environment so that it may serve the short-term and long-term needs of the Filipino people.

6   To put an end to foreign control over natural resources.[15]

These principles were carried over to the People's Agrarian Reform Code (PARCODE) adopted by CPAR in June 1988 after the failure of the President and of Congress to enact a satisfactory agrarian reform law. According to Francisco Baltazar, chairperson of CPAR in April 1990, the aim is to gather some two million signatures for PARCODE, to give it the status of a people's legislative initiative. Among the more specific principles embodied in PARCODE are the distribution of land to agricultural workers, with compensation which takes account of their payment of rent and their contribution of unpaid labour; the inclusion of all agricultural lands in the reform; direct participation of the beneficiaries in the decision-making and implementation processes; an emphasis on cooperatives and other collective forms of farming; the recognition of the right of women to own land and of the right of indigenous peoples to their ancestral domains; just labour standards for agricultural workers; fisheries reform for fisherfolk; and Filipinisation of lands under the control of transnational corporations.

The impact of the rice crisis in mid-1990, triggered by the implementation of the Letter of Intent providing for deregulation and the removal of subsidies, led farmers' and rural workers' groups to see more clearly the links between their plight and the debt. Mass actions on the rice issue brought the three major groups – CPAR, SANDUGUAN, and the Federation of Free Farmers – together in a Peasants' Forum where more detailed alternative development strategies with emphasis on countryside issues are being discussed and worked out.

Women's voices
Women are another section of the population responding in a major way to the debt crisis, as well as articulating an alternative development strategy with more specific concerns. The National Congress on Women and Debt, held in July 1989 under the co-sponsorship of the Freedom From Debt Coalition, OXFAM, and women's organisations, exposed the fact that 'The debt crisis and the resulting structural adjustment policies have made more women poor, have made poor women poorer, and made women poorer in relation to men.'[16] The Congress brought together the major women's groups, among them GABRIELA, Civic Assembly of Women in the Philippines, KaBaPa and PILIPINA.

In subsequent meetings and conferences, major women's organisations, working under the Group of 10 and the Women's Action Network for Development (WAND), hammered out strategies for 'women in development'. These address the gender-specific disadvantages of women, advocate access to education, training, funding, and technology, call for greater participation of women in political and decision-making processes, and stress that they must be empowered in the home, in the workplace, and in society in general, at the same time as they are involved in larger movements for structural transformation. Implicit in these strategies is the recognition of women's work and women's role, often invisible, under-valued, abused and overused in a debt-ridden social order.

The green perspective
The expanding environmental movement has also provided valuable inputs to the process of defining an alternative development strategy, with emphasis on its sustainability. According to Maximo T. Kalaw Jr., president of Haribon Foundation Inc and of Green Forum-Philippines (a broad coalition of non-governmental organisations, people's organisations, religious groups, and academic and research institutions), there have been shifts in concepts of economic development as expressed in various models. Previous models stressing economic growth, employment, equity and basic needs, without considering the needs of people and the environment, ended in failure. The latest model emphasises the role of the community and the power of individual people in providing for a better quality of life for all in harmony with the ecosystem.

Green Forum has a number of concrete proposals on the debt crisis: 'The shifting of debt servicing funds to development through a debt-for-development swap, the shifting of official development assistance (ODA) funds from military and government infrastructure spending to funding community capability building by NGOs [Non-Governmental Organis-ations], and the conversion of poor countries' debts to 'Common Futures' indemnity bonds for an NGO, PO [People's Organisations] development fund.'[17]

According to Maximo Kalaw, the poor, who are most affected by environmental degradation, comprise the natural constituency of the green movement. Among them are the 'four million tribal people affected by the logging policy, 18 million people squatting in the uplands, and two million fishermen marginalised from coastal fishing grounds'.[18] They are in the best position to manage and protect the resources from which they derive their sustenance and livelihood.

Thus, Green Forum advocates 'the recognition of tribal land rights and the inclusion of tribal people in the management of protected areas, and an immediate ban on logging of all virgin forests and the transfer of the rights to forest resources to upland communities'.[19] According to Maximo Kalaw, 'Poverty is the biggest despoiler – but to break that, we must use the resource wisely so that the poor benefit, so that they don't become poorer and destroy the resource.'[20]

In sum, the alternative development vision of the Green movement is 'community-based, equity-led, focused on community needs and well-being, decentralised, democratised and globalised, pro-people, pro-nature and pro-future'.[21]

The debt crisis has indeed prompted a broad spectrum of social forces in the Philippines to rethink development questions and provide alter-native answers. The hope is that in the healthy interchange of views, a decisive 'freedom from debt constituency' will emerge as a major component of a solid people's movement for alternative development.

12

The need for international cooperation

In a statement made in Zambia in May 1989, Pope John Paul II made an urgent plea for international action on behalf of debt-ridden countries like the Philippines:

> The problem of international debt is a clear example of the inter-dependence which characterises relations between countries and continents. It is a problem which cannot be solved without mutual understanding and agreement between debtor and creditor nations, without sensitivity to the real circumstances of indebted nations on the part of the creditor agencies, and without a wise and committed policy of growth on the part of the developing nations themselves. Is it merely a rhetorical question to ask how many infants and children die every day in Africa because resources are now being swallowed up in debt repayment? There is no time now to lament policies of the past or those elements in the international financial and economic picture which have led to the present situation. Now is the time for a new and courageous international solidarity, a solidarity not based on self-interest but inspired and guided by a true concern for human beings.

The debt has become a moral and ethical issue. Church leaders of the Philippines, United States, Brazil and other Latin American countries have argued against continued payments which punish the poor, who have received no benefit from loans often made by corrupt and dictatorial governments.

The search for just and lasting solutions to the debt problem is being pursued more vigorously than previously. The Baker Plan, proposed in 1985 by the then US Treasury Secretary, advocated new lending by the creditors, so that debtor countries could 'grow out' of their debts. This was tried until 1988, but the multilateral banks did not have enough resources, and the commercial banks were reluctant to lend new money to heavily indebted states.[1] The next US Treasury Secretary outlined the Brady Plan in early 1989, which urged the banks to 'write off a portion of Third World debts, pass the benefits of secondary market discounts on to debtors, and grant temporary waivers on the payment of interest and principal for up to three years'.[2] Because the Plan relies on the voluntary efforts of commercial banks and total resources committed to it so far have not been large, its chances of success seem to be limited.

Clearly, partial and piecemeal strategies such as the Baker and Brady Plans cannot provide effective and lasting solutions. A comprehensive, international approach is needed, which brings not only the creditor banks and debtor governments into the picture, but also non-governmental and people's organisations in both lending and borrowing countries. This approach could include not only debt relief but also writing off fraudulent loans, revising the conditionalities for new lending, and engaging in 'debt swaps' linked to developmental and environmental objectives.

Campaigning against fraudulent loans

If debtor countries like the Philippines are to be allowed to 'selectively disengage' from fraudulent loans, international cooperation will be necessary. One lawyer-academic advocating 'selective disengagement' cautions that those wishing to pursue this idea must do their homework. He urges that they not only 'study from a legal perspective all the loan, credit and other debt agreements contracted by the Philippines, examine the terms and conditions of each, and determine how all of them relate together', but also (and more importantly), 'They must gather evidence and witnesses to support allegations of corruption, fraud and other irregularities'.[3]

International cooperation is necessary to prove, document, and publicise fraudulent loans, in order to bring to public attention the fact that forced payments for these loans are punishing debtor countries, while lending institutions in creditor countries which facilitated these loans are not held responsible. One example of cooperation along this line was the recent attendance of Dr Emmanuel de Dios, board member of the Freedom From Debt Coalition, in the stockholders' meeting of a major Swiss bank to expose the role of this bank in the Bataan nuclear plant case. His intervention was made possible by the Berne Declaration, a non-governmental organisation focusing on the debt issue, and other groups in Switzerland.

Dialogue with the International Monetary Fund

According to the Freedom From Debt Coalition, the IMF itself must take a position on fraudulent loans, because insisting on payment of these loans 'for which lenders are equally responsible is without moral bases'. This point is included in a paper submitted by the FDC to Michael Camdessus, the head of the IMF. The FDC also stressed that 'the IMF must introduce a change in its current orientation which is biased for short-term solutions (with very painful consequences) to the global debt crisis'; that 'the IMF must provide for popular participation in the structural adjustment processes'; and that 'the IMF must take action on BOP [Balance of Payments]-surplus countries who are raising tariff barriers on the products of debt-ridden countries'.[4]

The FDC argues strongly that 'international action on structural adjustment policies implemented as part of debt packages' should be 'brought to bear on the multilateral institutions'.

Debt swaps

Still another sphere of international cooperation relates to 'debt forgiveness schemes' and 'people-oriented debt-swap arrangements'. FDC emphasises that such swaps should be undertaken only after fraudulent loans have been disaggregated from the total, so that only legitimate loans are finally swapped.

UNICEF has led the call for a more 'people-sensitive approach to adjustment', which it claims is 'more than a matter of economic good sense or political expediency' because 'ultimately, it rests on the ethic of human solidarity, of concern for others, of human response to human suffering'.[5] This approach is based on the belief that even while working within the present international economic order, adjustment could be more growth-oriented and could ensure that the human needs of the poor and vulnerable would be protected.

In terms of a workable debt-swap arrangement, UNICEF, jointly with the Philippine government, has drawn up a proposal, entitled 'Debt Relief for Child Survival', for consideration by commercial banks and bilateral donors. Under the proposal, the forgiven debt would be donated to UNICEF in local currency for use in its child welfare programmes in Mindanao.[6]

Another initiative along this line is the 'Debt for Nature Swap'. In the Philippine case, the World-Wide Fund for Nature (USA) bought $2 million worth of debt, which, after being redeemed by the Central Bank in local currency, would be channelled to conservation projects jointly approved by Haribon Foundation Inc, the Department of Environment and Natural Resources (DENR), and WWF.[7]

The DENR itself has worked out a proposal on 'Debt Forgiveness for Forest Protection' which involves 'the condonation of portions of Philippine debt to multilateral and bilateral creditors in exchange for a Philippine commitment to preserve its tropical forests'. Accordingly, 'the transactions will be recorded as an inflow of grants to the country and the outflow of an equivalent amount of debt payments'.[8]

For their part, non-governmental organisations within Green Forum are talking about converting debts into 'Common Future' indemnity bonds which could go into a development fund for environmental causes. Through such efforts, Philippine forests expected to disappear within this decade may yet be saved.

One important area still to be explored is a debt-for-agrarian reform scheme. Only genuine agrarian reform can prevent the landless rural poor and the marginalised upland farmers from encroaching farther into forest lands.

Still another possibility is a debt-swap scheme to benefit women. Through such a scheme, resources from abroad would go to programmes and projects to help Filipino women minimise if not overcome the severe impact of the debt on themselves, their households, and their children.[9]

13

Conclusion: How the creditors could help

We have seen what a devastating impact the debt problem has had and continues to have on the possibility of genuine development in the Philippines, and particularly on the lives of the poor majority of the population. This is an intolerable state of affairs, which the creditors, if they worked together to find a solution, could do much to relieve.

Priorities: debt or people?

Debt reduction is essential to alleviate poverty and suffering. A useful starting point would be for all the creditors, whether banks, governments, or multilateral institutions, to accept (and let it be known to the authorities in the Philippines) that expenditure on the essential needs of the poor should come before debt-service payments. They might consider that prompt and full loan repayment at the expense of sustainable development, and in particular of social and infrastructural items, is counterproductive, in that it stifles productivity and growth, and thus the existence of a prosperous and rewarding partner for the future. It would help if they agreed to measures that would reduce the outflow of funds from the Philippines to a level compatible with social and environmental needs.

Reducing outstanding debt and current payments

A significant amount of debt could be written off in a discriminating manner. A starting point could be loans which involve fraud, corruption, or incompetence, such as loans for the Bataan nuclear power plant. These doubtful loans may total up to six billion dollars.[1] The corruption surrounding these loans, if it was not known to the lenders, certainly should have been.

Northern governments can accelerate the process of reducing commercial bank loans by pressing the need on the banks, as well as by specific action. The banks have started setting aside large provisions against possible bad debts owed by Third World countries, but generally without actually reducing the debt. Changes in the tax regulations such that banks can only claim tax advantages when the debt is actually written off, as recommended by OXFAM to the UK Treasury and Civil Service Select Committee, would be helpful here. Another useful move would be to encourage banks, and indeed export credit agencies holding official debt, to reduce the recognised value of the debt to reflect its market value, rather than its unrealistic face value. For this they could use a variety of market-related mechanisms; a recent proposal was for the US government, through bonds, to guarantee repayment of some of the debt by the Philippine government. Governments would not need to underwrite the international financial system, since it is now clear that there is no serious threat posed to Northern banks as a group by large-scale debt write-offs.

Debt reduction or write-off is needed from official as well as commercial creditors (the Philippines debt is split nearly evenly between these two categories). The massive write-offs of Polish and Egyptian debt announced in May 1991 show that this is feasible where there is the will.

A very positive step would be for Northern governments to agree to a cap on debt-service payments as a percentage of visible export earnings. If, in addition, Northern countries opened up their markets to Philippine exports, this would result in increased foreign exchange earnings, and so a capacity to increase debt repayments. It is only reasonable for the Northern countries themselves to heed the trade liberalisation advice which they consistently urge on the Philippines. A moratorium for a period on debt service, especially on payments on the loans being investigated for possible fraud, is another measure which banks might accept without resistance if it is put forward by the government of the Philippines. The Brady Plan was the expression of an international consensus that debt reduction is a pressing necessity. In the light of this, it would help if the creditors treated any moves by the Philippines government to reduce debt service not as hostile acts, but rather as signals of the need to reopen negotiations for easier terms.

Some other measures
Beyond this there is a range of measures that could be deployed as appropriate by the various types of creditors. Governments could provide more aid, and more of the concessionary rather than the tied type of aid. (Some aid from Japan has required as much as 90 per cent to be spent on Japanese goods, according to a study by the National Economic and Development Authority.[2]) More could be provided in the form of grants rather than loans, and loans could be converted into grants. It would help if debt relief were not made conditional on the government pursuing economic policies which are likely to erode even further the living

standards of the poor. It would be necessary for official debt relief to come from additional funds, not from existing budgets. Multilateral bodies could offer more assistance, both financial and technical, with easier interest and repayment terms.

Other helpful technical measures would be the conversion of out-standing debt from floating to fixed interest rates, and readiness on the part of creditors to accept payment in kind.

Debt reduction for development and social needs

Especially worthy of consideration are imaginative ways of reducing debt by converting it into funds for activities furthering development and meeting social needs, such as the UNICEF 'Debt Relief for Child Survival' scheme and the World Wide Fund for Nature 'Debt for Nature Swap' mentioned earlier. These are similar to the debt-for-conservation scheme recently adopted in Costa Rica (though it should be remembered that these swaps are to be promoted only if the activity to be funded as a result is both socially and environmentally sound). This approach to debt reduction is in the spirit of the agenda of the Northern countries as formulated, for example, in a statement from the 1989 summit meeting of the Group of Seven industrial nations.

In view of the severe and accelerating environmental degradation described earlier, a measure along these lines that would be especially appropriate to the Philippines would be debt reduction to assist the process of agrarian reform. Although inequitable development and human greed have both contributed greatly to the environmental deterioration, the debt crisis has made it much worse. This has occurred both through the over-exploitation of natural resources to generate foreign exchange (for example, through cash cropping and fish farming for export, as described earlier) as well as through the unsustainable economic activities (slash-and-burn agriculture in forests, and unsustainable fishing, for instance) to which the poor have been driven by the impact at household level of general economic pressures.

It does not follow, however, that debt reduction by itself would directly alleviate the environmental problem; nor would devoting funds to environmental policing be an adequate solution. On the other hand, using local currency funds made available by debt reduction (funds which otherwise would have been spent in hard currency on debt service) to acquire land for redistribution in a genuine agrarian reform programme would tackle one of the roots of the problem, reducing and hopefully reversing the exodus of farmers from the lowlands to slash-and-burn farming in the upland forest regions. The government has hitherto been hampered by lack of funds as well as by political constraints in attempting to implement the land reform to which it is officially committed. Debt reduction could both supply the missing funds and constitute a plum that would make the associated land reform more politically acceptable.

Besides having a positive environmental impact, land reform, as shown by experience elsewhere in South East Asia, could be expected to raise productivity per hectare, and provide the basis for a broadly-based internal market to support appropriate industrialisation, as occurred in Taiwan and South Korea.

Consideration of the environment and agrarian reform highlights the fact that the debt problem is only a part, albeit a vital part, of the overall question of the future course of development in the Philippines, and a constructive resolution of the debt problem requires it to be seen in this broader perspective. This brings us immediately to the question of the lending to the Philippines by the multilateral institutions, principally the IMF and the World Bank (WB), and particularly the conditions attached to these loans.

IMF/World Bank conditionality

The International Monetary Fund was originally set up to deal with short-term balance of payment imbalances, with a time horizon of about one year. Though it now cooperates with the World Bank in programmes with a broader scope and longer time horizon, a continued proclivity for stringent, narrowly-focused measures appears very clearly in the recent (September 1990) memorandum of its review mission to the Philippines, entitled 'The Philippines: Outline of a Stabilization Programme, 1991-1992'. The suggestions of that document, which are harsher than those of the Letter of Intent, are largely incorporated in the government's new 'Philippine Economic Stabilization Program'. These include a quick, sharp reduction in the fiscal deficit, monetary targets that will promote economic contraction, and, as its main revenue-raising measure, a 7 per cent import levy (since raised to 9 per cent), while omitting measures to cushion the effect of this latter step on the poor, on whom it will impact particularly strongly.[3] The package strongly resembles the drastic 1984 IMF programme which, while markedly reducing inflation and the budget and balance of payments deficits, also contributed to a catastrophic fall in investment, record levels of unemployment and underemployment, and a fall in real per capita income by 1985 to the levels of ten years previously.[4]

In the past, the IMF has required excessively harsh measures, exclusively geared to the balance of payments but having a catastrophic effect on a whole range of domestic economic factors and on the welfare of the people. It is required *not* to do so by its own articles of association, and recent very welcome statements by its managing director, Michel Camdessus, have pledged greater IMF attention to social and environmental concerns. The IMF could help by allowing a longer period for any adjustment, and make the level of adjustment commensurate with the resources available to the Philippines, after allowing enough for expenditures on infrastructure, vital social programmes, and reasonable sustainable growth.

While the IMF and the World Bank both acknowledge the need for a case-by-case approach in designing countries' programmes, their recommendations for the Philippines appear to ignore the specific social and developmental needs of that country. They comprise all the elements familiar from many other IMF/WB programmes: indiscriminate decontrol, devaluation, liberalisation of trade and inward investment, and reduction in budget deficits and in the role of government. Whatever the virtues of some or all of these measures in particular circumstances, they are not all appropriate for every country at every time. With regard to the Philippines, it is instructive to compare the IMF/WB programmes with development in the 'four tigers' of South East Asia (South Korea, Taiwan, Hong Kong, and Singapore), which it is sometimes suggested the Philippines should attempt to emulate. These countries, contrary to what is sometimes asserted, did not achieve their remarkable growth through indiscriminate liberalisation and *laissez-faire* economic policy. South Korea and Taiwan, for example, both built up their industrial bases by carefully planned governmental nurturing of selected industries, using subsidies and protectionist measures to foster their development until they were able to compete in the international arena, in which they have since proved so successful.[5] From a Philippine viewpoint it is also significant that in both countries genuine and thorough-going land reforms played an essential role in their progress.

If the IMF and World Bank set conditions that make development impossible, the misery of the poor is only intensified. As this book has tried to show, the single factor most severely inhibiting any sort of economic development is the constant drain on resources through debt-service payments, yet the IMF and WB have not recommended that the government reduce its payments.

The level of budget cuts required leaves no resources for vital expenditure on infrastructure, such as transport, communications, energy, and flood control, thus discouraging private investment; or on basic health and education items, thus preventing the development of a skilled and effective labour force, as well as inflicting great suffering. So growth is thwarted. Is all this in accord with article 1(v) of the IMF Articles of Agreement, stating that correction of balance of payments imbalances should proceed 'without resorting to measures destructive of national or international prosperity', or with the IMF's more recent guidelines on conditionality, requiring it to give due weight 'to the domestic, social, and political objectives, the economic priorities and circumstances of members, including the causes of their balance of payments problems'?[6]

The major flaw of the IMF/WB programmes for the Philippines has been their generally disastrous impact on the lives of the poor, as documented throughout this book. The Letter of Intent promises 'poverty alleviation', but we have seen how this works out in practice, and, very significantly, this is not one of the criteria employed in the IMF's six-monthly reviews of implementation of its programme.

There are several significant ways in which the IMF and World Bank might help to relieve the pressure on the poorest people of the Philippines. They include the following:

- Not insisting on levels of debt service that destroy any possibility of growth and development; at present, the latter are treated as residuals, with debt service given absolute priority.

- Avoiding measures that result in further impoverishment of the poor. All conditionality could include measures to shelter the poor from any adverse effects on their already desperate plight, and the implementation and effectiveness of these measures would need to be regularly and carefully monitored.

- Guarding against indiscriminate, uncontrolled access (or even special favours) for multinational corporations, where in the view of the Philippine government this would be likely to lead to adverse effects such as environmental damage, obstruction of technology transfer, massive foreign exchange outflows, or prevention of the development of domestic industries.

- Recognising that genuine agrarian and urban land reform is vital to real, broad-based development in the Philippines, and promoting measures to advance it.

– Recognising that the State can play a valid role in guiding aspects of the development process, and that this may for a time require well-planned and carefully targeted subsidies and protectionist measures, as seen in other, successful South East Asian economies.

– In costing activities designed to provide foreign exchange from exports, taking full account of their environmental impact, so as to give a realistic picture of true economic costs.

– Speaking out more forcefully about the need for parallel adjustment measures in the North. At present, Southern countries are obliged to adopt any and every means to boost their exports, while the wealthy creditor countries erect ever greater barriers to access to their markets. The latter could help by adopting import liberalisation measures.

These changes would bring about a profound transformation for the better in IMF/WB programmes. In developing them, it would help if the IMF and the World Bank were open to discussion and consultation with non-government academics and with representatives of bodies speaking on behalf of the majority of the Philippine people. The need for such changes is urgent, if millions more lives are not to be wasted, and irreplaceable natural resources lost.

Notes

1   Introduction

1   Michael Duenas, 'The pathetic plight of Filipina workers abroad', *Philippines Free Press* (2 June, 1990).

2   Filomeno S. Sta. Ana, 'The Passion and Debt of the Filipino People', National Council of Churches in the Philippines (1989).

3   Ibid.

2   The origins of the problem

1   Cited in Leonor M. Briones, 'The Philippine External Debt: International Cooperation Toward a People – Centered Debt Strategy', paper presented to the US – Asia Institute, Philippine International Convention Center, 14 May 1990.

2   Actual figures for 1988, 1989, and 1990 are – 2.785 billion, – $1.929 billion, and – $2.179 billion, respectively. See 'Progress Report on the Philippine Agenda for Sustained Growth and Development, Program for the Mutilateral Aid Initiative (MAI)/Philippine Assistance Program (PAP)', January 1991.

3   Leonor M. Briones, 'The Continuing Debt Crisis and the Destruction of the Environment: Two Aspects of the Same Coin', unpublished paper, p. 11.

4   Alfredo R. Pascua, 'A hard look on our ills and tribulations', in *Sarilakas Grassroots Development*, IV, 1 and 2.

5   *Issues on the Philippines' Economic Dependence* (Quezon City: Ateneo de Manila Center for Social Policy and Public Affairs, 1989).

6   Renato and Letizia Constantino, *The Philippines: The Continuing Past* (Quezon City: Foundation for Nationalist Studies, 1978), p. 114

7   Cheryl Payer, *The Debt Trap* (Penguin Books, 1974) pp. 71 – 2.

8   Freedom From Debt Coalition, *Questions and Answers on the Philippine Debt Crisis*, n.d. For in – depth discussion on the role of the International Monetary Fund and the World Bank in the Philippine debt crisis during the Marcos period, see the following sources: Vivencio R. Jose, ed., *Mortgaging the Future – The World Bank and IMF in the Philippines* (Quezon City: Foundation for Nationalist Studies, 1982); Walden Bello,

David Kinley and Elaine Elinson, *Development Debacle: The World Bank in the Philippines* (San Francisco: Institute for Food and Development Policy, 1982); and Robin Broad, *Unequal Alliance, 1979 – 1986, The World Bank, the International Monetary Fund, and the Philippines* (Quezon City: Ateneo de Manila University Press, 1988).

9   *Issues on the Philippines' Economic Dependence*, op. cit.

10   Leonor M. Briones, 'An Overview of the External Debt Problem', paper presented at the National Congress on Women and Debt, University of the Philippines School of Labor and Industrial Relations, 23 July 1989.

11   Leonor M. Briones, 'The Philippine debt burden: who borrows? who pays?' in *International Debt Crisis: Focus on the Philippines* (Quezon City: International Studies Institute of the Philippines, 1984).

12   Leonor M. Briones, 'The Impact of External Debt and Adjustment Policies on the Realization of the Right to Development as a Human Right', paper presented at the Global Consultation on the Realization of the Right to Development as a Human Right, United Nations Centre for Human Rights, Geneva, 8 –12 January 1990.

13   Merlin M. Magallona, 'The Philippine debt crisis in an international setting', in *International Debt Crisis: Focus on the Philippines* (Quezon City: International Studies Institute of the Philippines, 1984).

14   Freedom From Debt Coalition, *Questions and Answers on the Debt Crisis*, n.d.

15   Briones, 'The Philippine debt burden: who borrows? who pays?', op.cit.

16   Roberto Verzola, Mae Buenaventura, and Edgardo Santoalla, 'Research on the Philippine Nuclear Power Plant Loans – Summary, Conclusions and Recommendations', paper presented during a press conference at the National Press Club, 23 August 1990.

17   Freedom From Debt Coalition, *Questions and Answers on the Philippine Debt Crisis*, n.d.

18   Cited in Briones, 'The Philippine External Debt: International Cooperation Toward a People – Centered Debt Strategy', op.cit.

19   Cited in Emmanuel S. de Dios and Carlos C. Bautista, 'Of Cabbages and Kings – Analyzing the Economy in the 1990s', paper delivered at an FDC forum with businessmen, 13 February 1990. Actual debt service for the years 1989 and 1990 amounted to more than $4 billion annually.

20   *Issues on the Philippines' Economic Dependence*, op. cit. A new LoI was approved by the IMF in early 1991. It will result in higher prices because of the imposition of a nine per cent import levy, steeper electricity rates because of the removal of government subsidy to the National Power Corporation, and even more taxes to achieve a revenue of P20 billion.

21 Solita Collas – Monsod, *Debt or Development: Philippine Imperatives and the Conventional Strategy for Debt Management*, Discussion Paper No. 8916, University of the Philippines School of Economics, October 1989.

22 Merlin M. Magallona, *US Marshall Plan for the Philippines: US Military Bases and Foreign Monopoly Capital* (Quezon City: New Horizons Research and Publications, 1989).

23 Monsod, op.cit.

3   What the debt means to the poor

1 Table 7, 'Incidence of poverty in the Philippines and NCR 1985 and 1988', in Ponciano Intal, 'Trends on poverty, income distribution, development of domestic markets and economic growth in the Philippines', in *Economic Growth and Income Distribution* (Manila: Friedrich Ebert Stiftung, 1989).

2 *Ibon Facts and Figures*, Vol XI, No. 24 (31 December 1988).

3 Intal, op.cit., p. 120.

4 UNICEF, *Adjustment with a Human Face* (Oxford: Oxford University Press, 1987) p. 33.

5 Ibid., p. 34.

6 Karina Constantino – David, 'Access of the poor to basic social services', in *Poverty and Growth in the Philippines* (Manila: Friedrich Ebert Stiftung, 1989), p. 34.

7 Tentative figures based on Table II. B. I, 'National Government Expenditures by Department – Special Purpose Fund 1976–87', Department of Budget and Management.

8 Constantino – David, op.cit., p. 36.

9 Ibid.

4   Health: a life or debt question

1 John Canavagh and Robin Broad, 'Repaying RP debt kills a Filipino child per hour', *Philippine Daily Inquirer* (30 March 1989).

2 Michael Lim Tan, Susan Pineda and Ma. Concepcion Alfiler, 'The DOH budget: aiming for efficiency and equity?' in *Health Alert* 100 (December 1989).

3 Filomeno S. Sta. Ana III, 'Philippine Foreign Debt and its Social Impact', paper presented at International Forum: Economic Growth and Income Distribution in the ASEAN Region (28 November 1989).

4 Department of Health, 'Sectoral Implications of MEP and the Proposed Programs of Action to Minimize the Costs of Adjustment', unpublished (1989).

5 Leonor M. Briones, 'Pagliliwanag sa mga Isyu ng Pagkakautang', Papers and Proceedings of the National Congress on Women and Debt (23 July 1989).

6 Sta. Ana, op.cit.

7 'Ensuring the people's right to health', *Philippine Currents* (June 1986).

8 Jose Tamayo, M.D. Position Paper, Proceedings of the Fourth Annual Convention of the Philippine Chamber of Health, Manila, 8 – 9 June, 1989.

9 Interview with Dr Orville Solon, University of the Philippines School of Economics, 17 April, 1990.

10 Report of the Senate Committee on Health, Series No. 1 (1989), p. 21.

11 Bernard Karganilla in 'Health (What makes the Filipino sick?)', *Education Forum – TAP*, VIII, SM 135 (30 June 1988).

12 Josefa S. Francisco, 'Fact Sheet on Filipino Women', Women's Resource and Research Center, Quezon City (1988).

13 'Ensuring the people's right to health', op.cit.

14 Alejandro N. Herrin, 'Access to basic services and the efficiency of public provision: The case of health care service in the Philippines', in *Economic Growth and Income Distribution* (Manila: Frederich Ebert Stiftung, 1989).

15 Ofelia P. Saniel and Jane C. Baltazar, 'The health status of Filipina women and risks to their reproductive health', in *Women and Health Book* Series No. 2, Institute for Social Studies and Action, Quezon City (1989).

16 Aida Fulleros Santos and Lynn F. Lee, *The Debt Crisis – Treadmill of Poverty for Filipino Women* (Quezon City: Kalayaan, 1989), p. 31.

17 Martin J. de la Rosa II, 'Induced Abortion: Is it Really a Problem?', National Conference on Safe Motherhood (September 1987), Department of Health (1988), p. 41.

18 Interview with Michael Tan, HAIN office, Philam, Quezon City, 12 February 1991.

5   Education: down from number one

1 Leonor Briones, 'Pagliliwanag sa mga Isyu ng Pagkakautang,' National Congress on Women and Debt, 23 July 1989.

2 Interview with Benjamin Balbuena, office of the Alliance of Concerned Teachers, 4 May 1990.

3 Interview with Ed Escultura, University of the Philippines College of Science, May 1990.

4 Juan Alano, 'Not enough teachers, rooms this year', *Philippine Daily Inquirer* (3 June 1989), cited in *Teacher's Journal* (June–December 1989). For schoolyear 1990–91, DECS estimates teacher shortage at 14,905 for elementary level and 22,450 for high school level. Ceferino Acosta III and Sammy Santos, 'Classes begin today in public schools', *Philippine Daily Globe* (11 June 1990).

5 'Teacher shortage in Cebu seen', *Philippine Daily Inquirer* (7 May 1990).

6 Interview with Merlinda Anonuevo, office of the Manila Public School Teachers Association (MPSTA), Sampaloc Manila, 17 May 1990. Merlinda Anonuevo found herself jobless in late 1991, as a consequence of joining the four–week teachers' strike in September.

7 Interview with Vangie Ricasio, MPSTA office, Manila, 17 May 1990.

8 The most dramatic mass action – the four–week teachers' strike of September 1990 – resulted in the dismissal of 844 and the suspension of 2,000 others. Martha Victoria E. Cagurangan, 'Life after dismissal', *Sunday Globe* (3 February 1991).

6 Debt, labour, and employment

1 NEDA, 'Labor and employment indicators', *Economic Updates*, I, 2 (23 April 1990).

2 'Program for the Multilateral Aid Initiative (MAI)/Philippine Assistance Program (PAP), The Philippine Agenda for Sustained Growth and Development', Discussion Paper for the Pledging Session for the PAP in the Tokyo Meeting (July 1989), pp. 55–60.

3 Cayetano Paderanga, 'Is the coup playing a major role in the current performance of the economy?', *Daily Globe* (27 May 1990).

4 Rene E. Ofreneo, 'A Divided Economy, A Divided Labor Force and A Divided Labor Movement', professorial lecture, University of the Philippines School of Labor and Industrial Relations, Quezon City, 15 July 1989.

5 Bureau of Women and Young Workers, Philippines: National Monograph on Child Labor (4 September 1987) p. 2.

6 Rene E. Ofreneo, 'Structural Adjustments and Emerging Labor Deployment Patterns', paper presented to the University of the Philippines Research Program on the State of the Nation, January 1990.

7 Maragtas S.V. Amante *et al.*, 'Living Wage Standards for Industrial
Sector Worker Households in the National Capital Region', University
of the Philippines School of Labor and Industrial Relations, 1988,
updated in 1990 (typescript, unpublished).

7   Debt and the agrarian crisis

1 Thus, in 1981, outgoing World Bank President Robert McNamara
announced that while 'the Bank has financed projects in virtually all
sectors of the economy, particular emphasis has been given to
agriculture, which has accounted for more than one – third of the total
Bank/IDA lending' (Robert S. McNamara, 'Report and
Recommendations of the President of the International Bank for
Reconstruction and Development to the Executive Directors on a
Proposed Loan to the Republic of the Philippines for a Sector Program
for Elementary Education', Washington DC, 4 June 1981, p. 8).

2 Rene E. Ofreneo, *Deregulation and the Agrarian Crisis* (Quezon City:
University of the Philippines Institute of Industrial Relations, 1987),
chapter 2.

3 Interview with Berting Manalus, Ambo Santos, Cora Manalus, and
Miling Dizon, Sta. Rita, Cabiao, Nueva Ecija, April 1990.

4 As a land – reform measure, CARL is widely considered to be half –
hearted, because it seems to serve the interests of landowners and
agribusiness more than those of the peasantry and agricultural workers.
This is evidenced by its slow phasing, lack of material support,
adherence to 'fair market value' in the pricing of land, and its many
exemptions and loopholes that landowners could use to evade land
transfer.

5 Interview with leaders of various farmers' organisations belonging to
the Peasants' Forum, University of the Philippines School of Labor and
Industrial Relations, April 1990.

6 Cited in 'Crisis after crisis', *Philippine Currents* (April 1990).

8   Debt and the fishing communities

1 Caesar R. Biruin and Alfredo Pascua, 'Philippine fisheries: what's the
catch?', *Philippine Currents* (October 1989).

2 Alfredo R. Pascua, 'A hard look on our ills and tribulations', *Sarilakas
Grassroots Development*, Vol.IV, Nos. 1 and 2.

3 'Aquaculture and the subsistence fisherfolk', in *Lundayan*, Vol.1, No.1
(April – June 1990). In fact, the tenth OECF loan, consisting of five billion
yen, was for the Agro – Industrial Technology Transfer Program (AITTP),

a large chunk of which (32 per cent or almost P170 million as of mid – 1989) went into financing prawn farms ('The top – down mechanism of agricultural development aid', in *AMPO Japan – Asia Quarterly Review* 21, 4).

4 'Aquaculture and the subsistence fisherfolk', op. cit.

5 Fact sheet, 'Coral Reefs', Haribon Foundation.

6 Aleli Bawagan, 'Laguna Lake for whom?', *Philippine Currents* (October 1989).

7 Pascua, op.cit.

8 Bawagan, op.cit.

9 Riza Faith C. Ybanez, 'Calabar: a mirage of progress', *Lundayan*, op.cit.

10 Tambuyog Development Center, 'A Critique of the Five – Year Fisheries Development Program', unpublished document.

11 Ibid.

12 Ibid.

13 Ibid.

14 'Fisherfolk response', *Philippine Currents* (October 1989).

15 Lim Ann Soon, 'Levels of Perception Among Laguna Lake Fishermen: The Case of Brgy. Looc, Cardona, Rizal', master's thesis presented to the University of the Philippines College of Social Work and Community Development (June 1989).

16 Mang Lupo is referring to foreign brand – name products produced under licence in the Philippines, and to imported products such as fruits being dumped on the local market and sold cheaply.

9 Debt and the tribal Filipinos

1 'Tribal Filipinos: a profile', in *Tribal Filipinos and Ancestral Domain – Struggle Against Development Aggression*, Quezon City: Tabak (1990) pp. xvii–xix.

2 Annex A in Ponciano L. Bennagen, 'Philippine cultural minorities: victims as victors', in Vivencio R. Jose, *Mortgaging the Future – The World Bank and IMF in the Philippines* (Quezon City: Foundation for Nationalist Studies 1982).

3 Annex B, ibid.

4 Ambrocio Manaligod, S.T.O. 'Displacement: a government strategy for development', in *Struggle Against Development Aggression*, op.cit.

5 'Dayandi: to the last drop', ibid.

6 Paul Valentin, 'The State of the Environment in the Cordillera' (typescript, 1987).

7 *ITAG Ecowatch* 1, 1 (July – September 1989).

8 Paul Valentin, op.cit.

9 Leonor M. Briones, 'The Continuing Debt Crisis and the Destruction of the Environment: Two Aspects of the Same Coin' (unpublished paper, 1990).

10 C.C. Consolacion and H.A. Francisco, 'Rural Poverty in Ethno Community: An Analysis', Highland Socio–Economic Research Institute Monograph Series No. 88 – 01, Benguet State University (1988).

11 Ibid.

12 'Itogon residents air complaints against Benguet Corporation's expansion program', *Northern Dispatch*, II, 6, (9 February 1990).

13 Rowie Severino, 'Open pit mining provokes confrontation', *Manila Chronicle* (21 January 1990).

14 'A Hidden US – Cordillera Relationship – Benguet Corp.'s Secretive but Super–Rich American Investors' (typescript, n.d., in CRC library collection).

15 'Even children work as pocket miners', *Northern Dispatch*, II, 12 (24 March 1990).

16 'Travails of women miners', *Northern Dispatch*, II, 10 (9 March 1990).

17 'Pocket miners buck orders to leave', *Northern Dispatch*, I, 2 (9 September 1989).

18 'Itogon officials urge cancellation of surface mining permits', *Northern Dispatch*, I, 9 (18 October 1989).

19 'Blasting destroys 12 houses, wounds one', *Northern Dispatch*, I, 12 (18 November 1989).

20 'Benguet Corporation told to pay damages for blasting', *Northern Dispatch*, I, 14 (1 December 1989).

21 'Itogon officials oppose surface mining', *Northern Dispatch*, II, 8 (23 February 1990).

22 'Military crackdown imminent on Itogon folk protesting open-pit mining', *Northern Dispatch*, II, 12 (24 March 1990).

23 Papers of the CECC Founding Congress (at CRC library).

24 Interview with leaders of the Luneta and Loakan Pocket Miners' Association, Benguet, 5 May 1990.

25 'Military crackdown imminent on Itogon folk protesting open-pit mining', *Northern Dispatch*, II, 12 (24 March 1990.)

10 Debt and the urban poor

1 Joseph Cortes, 'Tackling the squatters problem', *Manila Times* (28 May 1989).

2 Angelita Y. Gregorio Medel, *The Urban Poor and the Housing Problem* (Quezon City: Ateneo de Manila University Center for Social Policy and Public Affairs, 1989) p. 1.

3 Ibid., p. 2.

4 Ibid., p. 3.

5 National Housing Authority Annual Report 1988, p. 28.

6 Ibid., p. 27.

7 Ibid, p. 25.

8 For a more detailed account of the World Bank project in the Tondo offshore area, see Cheryl Payer, *The World Bank – A Critical Analysis* (New York: Monthly Review Press, 1982), pp. 326 – 42. See also Luzviminda B. Encarnacion, Naila A. Lopez and Ma. Corazon Lising, 'A case study on public borrowings and project development', in Vivencio R. Jose, ed., *Mortgaging the Future – The World Bank and IMF in the Philippines* (Quezon City: Foundation for Nationalist Studies, 1982).

9 Translated from the original Filipino, 'Pahayag ng mga Maralitang Sambayanan ukol sa Programang Lupa at Pabahay', Appendix C, in Gregorio-Medel, op. cit., p. 26.

10 Ibid., p. 16.

11 Leaders and members of MAKAMASA were interviewed by the author in MAKAMASA's office, Magsaysay Village, Tondo, Manila, May 1990.

11 Towards an alternative strategy for debt and development

1 Interview with Filomeno Santa Ana, Freedom From Debt Coalition office, April 1990.

2 FDC Minimum Program.

3 Strategic Plan of the Freedom From Debt Coalition, approved in its second congress, July 1990.

4   Freedom From Debt Coalition, 'The Memorandum on Economic Policy: Six Points of Opposition, Six Alternative Conditions'.

5   Roberto Verzola, Mae Buenaventura and Edgardo Santoalla, 'Research on the Philippine Nuclear Power Plant Loans – Summary, Conclusions and Recommendations', paper presented at a press conference, National Press Club, Manila, 23 August 1990.

6   Oxfam has given five small grants, totalling £17,912, to FDC over the last three years.

7   For an extended discussion on this, see *Confronting the Debt Problem – A Challenge to Democracy in the Philippines*, a publication of Ateneo de Manila University, Center for Social Policy and Public Affairs, July – September 1989.

8   Interview with Senator Alberto Romulo, Valle Verde, Pasig, 2 June 1990.

9   Senator Alberto G. Romulo, 'Towards an economic policy for the poor: focus on debt policy', *Philippine Journal of Industrial Relations*, 8, 1, 1990, pp. 65 – 6.

10   *Confronting the Debt Problem*, op. cit., p.63.

11   FDC Comments on Senate Bill No. 1178.

12   *Confronting the Debt Problem*, op. cit., pp. 84 – 6.

13   Leonor M. Briones, 'The Impact of External Debt and Adjustment Policies on the Realization of the Right to Development as a Human Right,' paper read during the global consultation of the UN Center for Human Rights, 8 – 12 January 1990.

14   *Confronting the Debt Problem*, op. cit., pp. 90 – 1.

15   'The people's agrarian reform program', *Philippine Currents* (June 1987).

16   Karen Tanada, 'Effects of the Debt Crisis on Women' (typescript, 1989). For more information, see also Leonor M. Briones, Rosalinda Pineda-Ofreneo and Karen Tanada, *Women Want Freedom from Debt – A Primer* (Quezon City: Foreign Debt Coalition, 1989), and Aida Fulleros Santos and Lynn F. Lee, *The Debt Crisis, A Treadmill of Poverty for Filipino Women* (Quezon City: Kalayaan, 1989).

17   'Creating a Common Future – Philippine NGO Initiatives for Sustainable Development' (Document of the Green Forum, n.d.).

18   Interview with Maximo Kalaw Jr., Green Forum Office, Makati, Metro Manila, 19 April 1990.

19   'Creating a Common Future', op. cit.

20   Interview with Maximo Kalaw Jr., 19 April 1990.

21 'Creating a Common Future,' op.cit.

12 The need for international cooperation

1 'The Debt Crisis' 3, Economic Development Series, United Nations Department of Public Information, September 1989.

2 Ibid.

3 Raphael Perpetuo M. Lotilla, 'Selective disengagement of foreign sovereign debts: some principles relevant to the Philippine dilemma', in *The Debt Trap: How to Get Out of It* (Quezon City: International Studies Institute of the Philippines, 1987) p. 10.

4 Freedom From Debt Coalition, position paper for submission to IMF Managing Director Michel Camdessus, 20 February 1990.

5 UNICEF Manila, *Adjustment with a Human Face – Selected Reprints* (1988).

6 Bituin Gonzales, 'Debt for children: The UNICEF experience', in *Papers and Proceedings of the National Congress on Women and Debt*, University of the Philippines School of Labor and Industrial Relations, July 1989.

7 The Haribon President's Report (February 1988 – February 1989).

8 Executive Brief on Foreign Debt and the Financing of Environmental Programs, p. 10.

9 See *Women Want Freedom from Debt – A Primer* (Quezon City: Freedom From Debt Coalition, 1989).

13 Conclusion: how the creditors could help

1 R.H. Green, 'Brady and the Philippines: what progress?', *IDS Bulletin*, April 1990.

2 Freedom From Debt Coalition, *Questions and Answers on the Philippine Debt Crisis*, p. 22, n.d.

3 S. Collas-Monsod, 'The IMF Stabilization Program: Implications for the Philippines'.

4 Ibid.

5 J. Toye, *Dilemmas of Development: Reflections on the Counter – Revolution in Development Theory and Practice* (Oxford: Basil Blackwell, 1987).

6 J. Gold, *Conditionality*, IMF Pamphlet Series, No. 1 (IMF, 1979).

Further reading

Bello, W. et al. (1982), *Development Debacle: The World Bank in The Philippines*, San Francisco: Institute for Food and Development Policy.

Boyce, James K. (1990), *The Political Economy of External Indebtedness: A Case Study of The Philippines*, Philippine Institute for Development Studies.

Broad, Robin (1988), *Unequal Alliance, 1979-1986: The World Bank, the International Monetary Fund, and The Philippines*,Quezon City: Ateneo de Manila University Press, and Berkeley: University of California Press.

Canlas, Miranda and J. Putzel (1988), *Land, Poverty and Politics in The Philippines*, London: Catholic Institute for International Relations.

Europe and Philippine Foreign Debt, London: Philippine Resource Centre, 1988.

Europe and The Philippines: Towards a New Relationship, Amsterdam: Transnational Institute, 1987.

Goodno, James B. (1991), *The Philippines: Land of Broken Promises*, London: Zed Books.

Hildebrand, Dale (1991), *To Pay is to Die: The Philippine Foreign Debt Crisis*, Davao City: Philippine International Forum.

UK Banks and Philippine Foreign Debt, London: Philippine Resource Centre, 1988.

World Bank, World Development Report 1991, Oxford: Oxford University Press.

(The Philippine Resource Centre (1-2 Grangeway, London NW6 2BW) has a comprehensive library of documents – including official Government papers and World Bank reports – on the subject of debt and structural adjustment. The library is open to researchers. Telephone 071 624 0270 for details.)

Useful addresses

PHILIPPINE INFORMATION NETWORK
(a network of Philippine information centres)

Philippine Resource Centre,
1-2 Grangeway, London NW6 2BW
tel: (0)71 624 0270; fax: (0)71 328 2003 (Mark 'for PRC'); E-mail: GEONET
GEO2:PRC

Philippine Resource Centre,
PO Box 5, Fitzroy, Victoria 3065, Australia

Philippine Resource Centre,
PO Box 40090, Berkeley, CA 94704, USA

Philippinenburo,
Postfach 250408, Sachsenring 2-4, 5000 Koln 1, Germany
tel: (0)221 324506; fax: (0)221 314711

FIDOC,
Nolensweg 8, 3317 LE Dordrecht, The Netherlands
tel: (0)78 185652

Charles Henri Foubert-Philippine Study Centre,
c/o Crocevia, Via Merulana 247, 00185 Rome, Italy
tel: (0)6 7316 841; fax: (0)6 737660

BRITISH ORGANISATIONS

Catholic Institute for International Relations,
Unit 3, Canonbury Yard, 190a New North Road, London N1 7BJ
tel: (0)71 354 0883; fax: (0)71 359 0017; E-mail: GEONET GEO2:CIIR

Christian Aid,
Interchurch House, PO Box 100, London SE1
tel: (0)71 620 4444; fax: (0) E-mail: GEONET GEO2

Commission for Filipino Migrant Workers,
St Francis Community Centre, Pottery Lane, London W11
tel: (0)71 221 0356

Oxfam,
Oxfam House, 274 Banbury Road, Oxford OX2 7DZ
tel: (0)865 311311; fax: (0)865 312600

Philippine Ecumenical Network,
24 Butterfield Road, Bassett, Southampton SO1 7EE

Philippines Support Group,
11 Goodwin Street, London N4
tel: (0)71 272 5317

Third World First,
232 Cowley Road, Oxford OX4 1UH
(0)865 245678

EUROPEAN CAMPAIGNS

Berne Declaration Group,
Quellenstr. 25, 8005 Zurich, Switzerland
tel: (0)1 2716434

Commission for Filipino Migrant Workers International Office,
Haarlemmerdijk 173, 1013 KH Amsterdam, The Netherlands, (0)20 254829

European Campaign on Debt and Development (Eurodad),
145 Avenue Road, Southampton SO2 1BD, England

**Forum on Debt and Development (Fondad), Noordeinde 107a, 2514
GE The Hague, The Netherlands**
tel: (0)70 653820

Philippine Development Forum (Phildev),
Paulus Potterstraat 20, 1071 DA Amsterdam, The Netherlands

PHILIPPINE ORGANISATIONS

Freedom From Debt Coalition,
c/o School of Labor and Industrial Relations, University of the
Philippines, Diliman 1001, Quezon City, The Philippines
tel: (0)2 976061 to 69; (0)2 995071 to 74, locals 4213 and 4804
(a national coalition of more than 100 organisations)

GABRIELA,
35 Scout Delgado, Diliman, Quezon City, The Philippines
tel: (0)2 998034
(a national coalition of women's organisations)

IBON Databank,
PO Box SM-447, Manila, The Philippines
tel: (0)2 600203 and 603983; E-mail: GEONET GEO2:IBON
(a socio-economic databank)

Kaibigan,
Room 501 Bercion Bldg., 1186 Quezon Avenue, Quezon City, The
Philippines
tel: (0)2 986142; fax: (0)2 521 7225
(a research and assistance organisation for Filipino migrant workers)

Philippine Centre for Policy Studies,
PO Box 6, University of the Philippines Post Office, Diliman, Quezon City
1101, The Philippines
(economic policy research centre)